THE **TUBE**

STATION TO STATION ON THE LONDON UNDERGROUND

HOMELIKE

UN ND

WEATHER PROOF

· OLIVER GREEN ·

Published in Great Britain in 2012 by Shire Publications Ltd,
Midland House, West Way, Botley, Oxford OX2 0PH, United Kingdom.
44-02 23rd Street, Suite 219, Long Island City, NY 11101, USA.

E-mail: shire@shirebooks.co.uk   www.shirebooks.co.uk

A CIP catalogue record for this book is available from the British Library.

Shire General no. 4.   ISBN-13: 978 0 74781 227 2

Oliver Green has asserted his right under the Copyright, Designs and Patents Act,
1988, to be identified as the author of this book.

Designed by Myriam Bell Design and typeset in Gill Sans and P22 Underground.
Printed in China through Worldprint Ltd.

12 13 14 15 16   10 9 8 7 6 5 4 3 2 1

COVER IMAGE
Poster artwork by Tom Eckersley for an exhibition on London Transport design, 1995.
It is based on an original 1930s night photograph of Boston Manor station tower, one
of Charles Holden's classic station designs for the Piccadilly line.

TITLE PAGE IMAGE
Homelike, Weather Proof. Underground publicity featuring an early version of the
iconic roundel symbol, 1911.

ACKNOWLEDGEMENTS
The author is grateful to London Transport Museum/TfL for providing the following
images: cover, pages 8, 10, 13 (top), 15, 16, 21, 23, 25, 27, 28, 30, 32, 33, 36, 39, 40, 46, 47,
48, 60, 69 (lower), 82 (top), 91, 92, 93, 100, 104, 106, 107 (top), 112, 113. Page 43 is
from Getty Images, page 64 from Crossrail and page 72 (lower) from the author's
collection. All other photographs were taken by Oliver Green between 2008 and 2012.

CONTENTS

150 YEARS UNDERGROUND

The London Underground system is one of the world's largest and busiest urban metros. From a modest Victorian steam railway 3.5 miles long with just six stations, it has grown and developed over 150 years into eleven modern electric lines covering more than 250 route miles and serving 270 stations across the capital. It is responsible for over 3.5 million passenger journeys a day, which added up to a record figure of 1.1 billion journeys in 2010–11, more than the total for the entire UK national rail network.

The Underground has an essential role in keeping London on the move and providing the vital travel arteries of the city. The famous features of the system, the red and blue roundel and the iconic Tube map, are recognised everywhere as key symbols of London, familiar guides and reference points to residents and visitors alike.

The entire environment of the Underground, both above and below ground, has a distinctive look and design about it that has evolved yet remained comfortly consistent throughout the twentieth century. In the twenty-first century, as part of Transport for London (TfL), the system has

Opposite: Welcome to the Tube. The main escalator shaft from the street entrance at Holborn, 2010. Opened in 1933, this rebuilt interchange station was fitted with modern escalators in the 1990s.

Modern art at
a heritage station.
A Platform for Art
exhibition by Japanese
pop artist Chiho
Aoshima in 2006 on
the walls of Gloucester
Road station, built
in 1868.

effectively grown to embrace the London Overground
network of suburban lines, with a complete orbital service
around the city in operation from 2012. The Docklands Light
Railway (DLR) has also developed over the last twenty-five
years from a cheap substitute for a new Tube into an essential
adjunct to the Underground in serving and regenerating east
and southeast London.

All three of these systems are now managed for the
Mayor of London by TfL as part of an integrated multi-modal
transport system for the capital. They all appear on the Tube
map and use the same cashless Oyster card ticketing system.

By 2018 new deep tunnels for Crossrail will be carrying mainline services from east to west below London. Technically Crossrail will not be part of the Underground, but all the new stations will have direct interchange with the Tube, and feel seamlessly integrated into London's familiar underground travelling environment.

Journeys and exploration on the Underground are almost like trips through time as well as space, although they rarely feel as though they are in chronological sequence. Different parts of the infrastructure have been enlarged, extended, opened, closed, abandoned and rebuilt almost continuously for 150 years, but never in a set order. You can still find stations and buildings from every one of those sixteen decades, reflecting the styles and design of each period, and the changes in London's fortunes, but it is a complex picture to piece together.

Contrasting Edwardian styles at South Kensington, 2012. On the left the arcade entrance to the Metropolitan & District station by George Sherrin (1907), still in daily use; on the right Leslie Green's Piccadilly Tube station building (1906), redundant since the 1970s.

More than seventy of the pre-war stations are now listed buildings, given statutory protection by English Heritage as an important part of the city's built environment. London Underground has the challenging task of maintaining and upgrading the Tube's historic features whilst keeping a busy transport system up to date and fit for purpose in the twenty-first century.

Since the late 1940s investment in new capital projects on the Underground has been modest and little was spent on new stations or refurbishment until the 1990s, when the Jubilee line extension brought a welcome return of high-quality architecture and design to the Tube. Some of these stations and other features will certainly become the listed buildings of the future, to be cherished as some of London's best modern public architecture.

Brixton Tube station, opened in 1971 as the southern terminus of the Victoria line. Refurbished and upgraded with improved access from 2001 and a dramatic new double height entrance façade designed by Chetwood Associates.

As a working system, none of it can remain unchanged. There is a constant need to modernise and improve capacity as use of the Tube continues to grow inexorably. The upgrade programme that has been under way for more than a decade now will have to continue for many years and will never really be finished. A sustainable city must constantly renew itself and without an evolving Tube, London would seize up.

This book is an introduction to the fascinating built environment of the Tube through what can be seen today for the price of a Travelcard. Even your daily commute may begin to appear in a new light when you look at its features more closely and see how they fit together.

The first section is a brief chronology of the Underground's development over 150 years. Section two is a series of journeys on the system through which aspects of that entire history can be glimpsed and explored. Although they are not part of the Underground itself, the DLR, London Overground and Crossrail are all included.

Purists will object that we have sometimes used the name 'Tube' to refer to the whole system when technically only the deep-level lines run in tube tunnels. Until about thirty years ago London Transport was always careful to distinguish between its 'surface' lines (the original steam underground lines of the Metropolitan and District) and the deep 'tube' electric lines opened after 1890. We have opted for common usage here.

The word has been in popular use and become capitalised since the opening of the Twopenny Tube in 1900. Nowadays both TfL and the Underground itself use Tube as shorthand for the whole system, though the nickname has remained unique to London. Nowhere else in the world has a Tube, and every other city's urban railway is called a subway or a metro. Both of these expressions were first used in London but only caught on when systems developed elsewhere. As a final point to confuse the issue, remember that more than half the London Underground network is above ground anyway.

East Finchley, where the Northern line joined the overground steam branch line to High Barnet and electric Tube services were introduced in 1939–40. The new London Passenger Transport Board station by Charles Holden and Leonard Bucknell, which replaced the old LNER station of 1867, is now a listed building.

HISTORY

1860–89: METROPOLITAN AND DISTRICT

When construction of the world's first underground railway began in 1860, London was already served by a series of long-distance mainlines to the capital built over the previous twenty-five years. Seven separate mainline termini had opened around the edge of London bringing passenger services from every direction to London Bridge (1836), Euston (1837), Paddington (1838/54), Shoreditch (1840), Fenchurch Street (1841), Waterloo (1848), King's Cross (1852) and Victoria (1860).

Every railway company wanted access to the centre of town, but only one of these stations (Fenchurch Street) was actually within the square mile of the old City which then, as now, housed the business district. Charles Pearson, the influential City solicitor and a prime advocate for the Metropolitan Railway, argued that rail routes to the centre would also have a wider social benefit by enabling residents of overcrowded inner areas to move out and become commuters. There is little evidence that this happened to the inner-city poor, but Pearson was convinced that railways could

Opposite: Poster by R. T. Cooper showing the transformation of the old City line, reconstructed and linked with the Hampstead Tube to create the Northern line with modern air-door tube trains, 1924.

have positive benefits for urban life rather than destroying the city's fabric as many feared.

Despite some half-hearted attempts by parliament and the City corporation to restrict extensions into the heart of the metropolis, there was a flurry of new construction in the economic boom of the 1860s. Mainline extensions from the south bridged the Thames to Charing Cross (1864), Ludgate Hill (1865), Cannon Street (1866), Holborn Viaduct (1874) and Blackfriars (1886). From the north and east, railways were extended and pushed through to Broad Street (1865), St Pancras (1868), Liverpool Street (1874) and finally, with the last mainline to London in the nineteenth century, Marylebone (1899). For a guide to these termini see the author's *Discovering London Railway Stations* (also from Shire Publications).

In the mid-nineteenth century, underground railways were being proposed both to link the overground termini together and to bring travellers closer to the centre of the city. It was also claimed that they offered a solution to the growing problem of traffic congestion in central London. By the 1850s it was already said to take as long to cross central London by cab as to make the journey from Brighton to the capital by train. The mainline railways were actually contributing to the problem by forcing their passengers to transfer on to horse-drawn omnibuses or cabs to complete their journeys.

Baker Street station in 1863, with a broad gauge Great Western steam train arriving from Farringdon Street.

Baker Street in 2010, with a Circle line train arriving at the same platform in the original brick tunnel built by cut-and-cover below the Marylebone Road.

One of the attractions of building an underground railway was that it could be achieved in central London largely without major property demolition. Most of the original section of the Metropolitan Railway route from Paddington to the very edge of the City at Farringdon was built along main roads by 'cut and cover'. A shallow cutting for the trackbed was dug along the road, supported on either side by brick retaining walls and then roofed over with girders and brick to create an artificial tunnel on which the road surface could be reinstated when the work was complete. The Circle line platforms at Baker Street show the results of this construction method better than any other station as the main structure here has remained unchanged for 150 years.

The pioneer underground railway opened between Paddington (Bishops Road) and Farringdon Street on 10 January 1863. At first it was operated by the Great Western on the Metropolitan's behalf but the two companies fell out in a matter of months and the Metropolitan was soon using its own rolling stock. The line was extended eastwards to Moorgate Street (1865) and at the western end, through a link to a new overground branch, from Paddington to Hammersmith (1864), later to become the Hammersmith & City, and now part of the Circle line.

London's second underground line, built by the Metropolitan District Railway, was opened between South Kensington and Westminster in 1868, then extended along the new Thames Embankment to Blackfriars in 1870 and a City terminus at Mansion House in 1871. The Metropolitan joined up with the District in west London with an extension from Paddington through Bayswater and Notting Hill, opened in 1868. The original plan had been for the two privately operated underground companies, which were built in the same way by engineer John Fowler, eventually to merge into one. For various reasons, including the notorious personal antagonism and rivalry between the two company chairmen, Sir Edward Watkin (Metropolitan) and James Staats Forbes (District), this never happened.

Gloucester Road station, newly completed in 1868. Most of this building still survives with a cleaned and renovated façade.

District Railway map
of London, 1895, with the
steam underground lines
of the Metropolitan and
District shown in red and
other railways in blue.

The Inner Circle was not completed until 1884, after which it was jointly worked in bad-tempered partnership by the two railways. A junction was also built at the same time near Whitechapel with the East London Railway (ELR), which had been opened through the Thames Tunnel in 1869 and extended northwards in the 1870s. The new link line enabled the Metropolitan and District to run underground services off the Inner Circle and over the ELR to New Cross.

During the boom years of the 1860s and 1870s suburban branches off the mainlines were constructed all over outer London, which allowed a series of local passenger services to be introduced by the various separate railway companies. This included an 'Outer Circle' service, revived in amended orbital form with new links as part of London Overground 150 years later. Some of the lines built through London's 'northern heights' at this time eventually became linked to the Tube network in the late 1930s as extensions to the Northern line.

In the late nineteenth century the Metropolitan and District Railways both found it more profitable to extend feeder branches through outer London, often in partnership with other companies, and avoid the costly completion of the Inner Circle. The District pushed westwards on the surface through Earl's Court, which became its principal hub station, with branches and connections giving access to Richmond (1877), Ealing Broadway (1899), Hounslow (1883) and Wimbledon (1889).

Meanwhile the Metropolitan built what became known as its 'extension line' running northwest from Baker Street, initially through St John's Wood to Swiss Cottage (1868). This railway was extended overground through West Hampstead and Willesden Green to Harrow (1880). While the District's suburban extensions were short, the Metropolitan under Watkin developed long-distance mainline ambitions. As he told the Metropolitan shareholders in July 1888, 'I do not intend to be satisfied, if I live a few years, without seeing the Metropolitan Railway the grand terminus for a new system of railways throughout England'. His dream of a rail network stretching from Manchester to Paris via the Metropolitan through London and a Channel Tunnel to France seemed impossible to his contemporaries, but was virtually in place a century later.

Within a few years the Metropolitan was running right through Middlesex into Hertfordshire and Buckinghamshire. It reached Rickmansworth (1887), Chesham (1889) and Amersham (1892), today the outer limit of London Underground services. In the 1890s Metropolitan passenger services operated through to Aylesbury and beyond to remote Verney Junction, with connections for the Midlands and beyond. It is 50 miles from Baker Street and was the furthest outpost of the Victorian steam underground. Quainton Road station, just down the line towards Aylesbury, has been restored and preserved as part of the Buckinghamshire Railway Centre.

Amersham station in 2010, opened by the Metropolitan in 1892. This has been the outer limit of London Underground electric services since 1961.

At the start of the twentieth century both the original London underground companies were about to be transformed by electrification and new management, which would take the railways on entirely new development paths and into new relationships with the emerging tube railways. Both the Metropolitan and the District also had an increasing impact on London's suburban growth and development, becoming successful commuter railways as well as a means of getting round and across central London below ground.

1890–1919: DOWN THE TUBES

Despite the initial popularity and heavy use of the original steam underground lines opened in the 1860s, they were not a financial success. The rivalry between the separate but permanently linked Metropolitan and District Railways held back the development of an integrated underground railway network for London. Although it was widely admired as an impressive engineering achievement, no other city in the world followed London in building an urban underground railway for more than thirty years, until Budapest and Glasgow opened lines in 1896.

By this time a second significant breakthrough in urban transit had been pioneered in London. This was the completion of the first deep-level electric underground line in the world, the City & South London Railway. The C&SLR opened in 1890 over the 3.5 miles between Stockwell in south London and King William Street in the City. It was based on three vital technological developments: an efficient method of tunnelling through the London clay; a safe and reliable means of vertical transit for passengers at deep-level stations; and a pollution-free system for powering the trains. The innovations applied to the C&SLR were tube tunnelling with shields, safety lifts and electric traction. It was the first time that all three had been combined.

Tube tunnelling was first developed by engineer Peter Barlow, who built the Tower Subway under the Thames in 1870. He used a cylindrical iron shield which worked like a giant apple corer. Miners excavated the earth at the tunnel face from inside the shield, which was forced forward into the clay by hydraulic rams. As it progressed the tunnel was lined with curved iron segments which made up a self-supporting tube: hence the name.

Postcard of a Greathead shield being used to dig the Piccadilly Tube tunnels, c. 1905.

The Tower Subway was in effect a miniature prototype for the first tube railway. It was only 2.3 metres in diameter, too small to take a train, although when it first opened a little railcar on a cable was used to carry passengers through the tunnel. This was removed after a few weeks and the subway became a pedestrian toll tunnel under the Thames, eventually closed to the public when Tower Bridge was opened nearby in 1894. The little stone entry kiosk can still be seen close to the main entrance of the Tower of London, but there is no underground access. Barlow's small pioneer tunnel is now used to take pipes and cables under the river.

The C&SLR was built by Barlow's contractor James Henry Greathead, whose name has been given to soft-ground tunnelling shields ever since. This became the standard method for building deep tunnels under London, where the clay subsoil is easy to excavate in this way, unlike the hard rock of Manhattan for example. Greathead started construction in 1886 with a shaft sunk from a pier in the Thames, assembling the shields at the bottom and digging the tunnels out below the river bed in both directions.

Steam trains could obviously not be used in deep tube tunnels with no ventilation. The original plan was to use cable haulage, but during construction it was decided to use electric traction. This was a real leap of faith as electric power was still at a very early developmental stage on surface railways and had never been used deep underground anywhere. The electrical installation, designed by the Hopkinson brothers from Manchester, was primitive but it worked. At first the generator plant could barely provide enough power for the trains, and it soon had to be upgraded. Nothing else was electrically powered: the original station lifts were hydraulic and the gloomy platform tunnels were lit by gas.

As company chairman Charles Mott admitted soon after the railway opened, 'We were the experimenters and made the City & South London line a little too small.' But in spite of its shortcomings the railway was a great success and a far more significant technological breakthrough than the original Metropolitan line had been thirty years earlier. Deep-level electric tube railways appeared to be the future of rapid

Stockwell, terminus of London's first tube, the City & South London Railway, opened in 1890. This station was later reconstructed twice and only Kennington, the next stop on the line, still has a surface building to this original design with a large dome, by Thomas Figgis.

transit in London, though they offered poor financial returns for investors. The greatest difficulty then, as now, was not in refining the technology but how to raise the finance for further tube schemes.

Between 1894 and 1907 six more electric Tube railways were built under central London, together with extensions at both ends to the original C&SLR. Largely because of the difficulties in raising funds and the battles between different promoters, the various projects were not finished in the order in which they were started. Dozens more never got off the drawing board, but at the end of this brief period of intensive development the West End and City were criss-crossed by a deep tube network. No more new lines were created under central London for another sixty years.

The line-opening sequence began with the short Waterloo & City (1898), then the Central London and C&SLR extensions (1900) and the Great Northern & City (1904). These were all independent operations, followed by the three lines of the Underground Electric Railways of London (UERL), the Bakerloo (1906), Piccadilly (also 1906) and Hampstead (1907).

Because of the high cost of construction, all but one of the Tubes were built in tunnels of small diameter, restricting their use to customised rolling stock; this has limited capacity ever since. Only the GN&CR was designed as a Tube big enough to take 'surface' size rolling stock. London Underground trains still come in two basic sizes today: 'surface' stock can be run

Central London Railway poster, c. 1905, showing the interior and exterior design of the original Twopenny Tube stations opened in 1900, all to a standard design by Harry B. Measures, best seen now at Holland Park.

on the Metropolitan, District and Circle lines but only smaller Tube stock can be used in the deep tunnels. The size contrast is best seen where surface and Tube trains share overground tracks, such as the Uxbridge branch or west of Hammersmith where the District and Piccadilly lines run alongside each other.

In 1900 the Central London became the first railway to cross the West End, running under the full length of Oxford Street to the Bank at the heart of the City. It originally had a flat fare of 2d and no class divisions, creating the novelty of a complete social mix. The railway soon referred to itself in advertising as 'The Twopenny Tube' and popular use of the term Tube, now used as a proper name, and shorthand for the whole system, dates from this period.

The UERL was a holding company set up in 1902 by American entrepreneur Charles Tyson Yerkes, whose 'combine' operation also purchased and electrified the District Railway and the London United Tramways in west London. Yerkes was already known as 'the traction king' in the United States, where he was the main promoter of electric streetcars and new elevated railways in Chicago. These modern forms of urban transit were well established there by the late 1890s, and Yerkes saw the opportunity to develop similar projects in London, the world's largest city at the time.

In 1902–5 Yerkes' financial syndicate built a giant Thames-side power station at Lots Road, Chelsea, which was to provide most of the electricity for the London Underground for the next hundred years. The three Yerkes Tubes (Bakerloo, Piccadilly and Hampstead lines) had standard features which followed American practice and engineering, giving London a distinctive and instantly recognisable Tube environment. Architecturally this was replicated above and below ground at more than forty new stations opened across the city in 1906–7. These stations were designed by architect Leslie Green as almost identical ox-blood tiled units on load-bearing steel frames, one of the first examples of system building on this scale. Most of them survive in daily use with many of their historic features renovated and modernised.

Nearly all the deep Tube stations had electric lifts, mostly American Otis designs, some of which were in use for eighty years. The first escalator on the Underground was installed by the UERL at Earl's Court in 1911, linking the District and Piccadilly line platforms. Similar 'moving staircases' were fitted to all new deep tube stations opened after this date.

The steam underground lines of the Metropolitan and District Railways, including the Inner Circle, were electrified in 1905 on the DC conductor rail system recommended by Yerkes' American electrical engineers, which had been tried and tested on his elevated lines in Chicago. In London a four-rail system was adopted with separate, insulated positive and negative

Oxford Circus Bakerloo UERL Tube station painted by architect Leslie Green in 1905, a year before the station opened on Argyll Street opposite the separate CLR station of 1900. Both façades survive, showing the contrasting standard designs of Green and Measures.

conductor rails, eventually to become standard on all London Underground lines. The District first trialled this electric working on its newly built branch line from Ealing to South Harrow in 1903, and a year later the Metropolitan was also

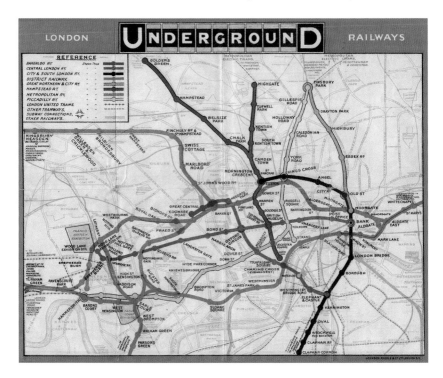

running its first electric trains on a new overground extension from Harrow-on-the-Hill to Uxbridge. But cooperation between the old rivals was still limited and the Met remained firmly independent of the UERL, rejecting a takeover bid.

Yerkes died in 1905, leaving his UERL group nearly bankrupt, but the company's fortunes revived with the arrival of Albert Stanley, the future Lord Ashfield, as general manager in 1907. Under Stanley's adroit leadership (he became managing director in 1910), the UERL expanded, taking over two of the original tube lines (the C&SLR and the CLR) as well as the main London bus company, the London General Omnibus Company. By 1913 the LGOC's fleet of new motor buses was providing coordinated feeder services to the Underground rather than road competition, and the first extension of the Bakerloo Tube had opened.

Stanley put his commercial manager, Frank Pick, in charge of planning and promoting these new developments, and the UERL soon got a reputation for its attractive publicity and design, especially through Pick's artistic poster commissions and clear signage. In 1908 the first distinctive station platform signs were introduced, large red enamel discs with the name in white on a blue cross bar. At the same time the first free pocket maps of the system were issued. Stanley and Pick were well aware of the benefits of strong marketing and helpful passenger information, both concepts that the established Victorian railway companies were slow to grasp.

Opposite: The first free, folding pocket map of the Underground, issued in 1908 as a joint marketing initiative by the separate companies. The next new Tube under central London, the Victoria line, was opened sixty years later.

An original blue bar and red disc enamel platform nameplate from Tufnell Park station. This early version of the UERL's distinctive symbol was first introduced in 1908.

The rival Metropolitan also appointed an ambitious new general manager in 1908. Robert Selbie started improving the newly electrified Met by rebuilding the hub station at Baker Street and double tracking much of the mainline, as well as acquiring the East London Railway and the Great Northern & City Tube. By 1913, when the Met celebrated its diamond jubilee, he was confidently maintaining the original underground company's independence. The First World War (1914–18) curtailed the expansion plans of both the UERL and the Met, though some new works continued under wartime conditions.

1920–39: SUBURBIA AND METRO-LAND

In 1919 both Underground companies dusted off their pre-war expansion plans. The UERL and the Met were ready to take advantage of the financial assistance now made available to them by the state. The government was anxious to reduce unemployment, boost the economy and encourage house building with 'homes fit for heroes' in post-war Britain. New suburban railways in Greater London could help stimulate these policies and were an essential element in the wider suburban development that followed in the 1920s. Although the UERL and the Met were both still private companies, government guarantees were offered on the loans they required for new capital projects, and this became a standard funding mechanism.

In 1922–6 the UERL completed a major three-part scheme to extend the Hampstead Tube at both ends, reconstruct the City & South London line and link the two together. In north London the Tube was extended overground from Golders Green to Edgware in 1922–4, and south from Clapham Common, in new tunnels to Morden, in 1924–6. In the centre the City line was rebuilt and linked to the Hampstead line via an elaborate four-way underground junction at Camden Town. This created the main part of the Northern line as it is today, a spinal north–south Tube right under London with a split route serving both the City and West End. The combined Hampstead and City lines were only renamed the Northern line in 1937.

In the late 1920s the UERL completed two major showpiece projects in central London, one below and the other above ground. Piccadilly Circus station, where the Bakerloo and Piccadilly lines crossed, was completely reconstructed to cope with the massive increase in passengers using this key station since opening in 1906. A large oval booking hall and circulation space was created directly below the famous intersection of Regent Street and Piccadilly, from which banks of escalators ran down to the platforms, replacing the original station lifts.

Opened in 1928, this was another stunning piece of civil engineering, but unlike the invisible Camden Town junctions, the UERL were able to show off and promote Piccadilly Circus as an inviting underground environment. Frank Pick, now promoted to managing director, was concerned about every aspect of the look and design of the Underground and insisted that it must appear modern, confident and 'fit for purpose'. He had brought in consultant architect Charles Holden to design the Morden extension station entrances and break away from Edwardian Tube-station design. The success of these modest but radical buildings led Pick to commission Holden for a more prominent project.

At Piccadilly Circus Holden took the idea of a Tube station one step further: he transformed what might otherwise have been a bleak engineer's hole in the ground into a welcoming public space at the heart of London. The new booking hall felt like an extension of the high-class shopping streets above, with what Holden called an 'ambulatory' featuring display showcases, marble and bronze fittings, and stylish decoration including murals over the escalators and a map of the world.

Postcard promoting the rebuilt Piccadilly Circus station, much admired internationally as the new hub of the Tube after complete reconstruction in 1925–8. Holden's oval booking hall and the new escalators particularly impressed the Russians, who took advice from London Underground when building the Moscow Metro in the 1930s.

Piccadilly Circus below ground soon became one of the sights of London. Among the admiring overseas visitors was a group of Soviet engineers planning a new metro for Moscow. This led to London Underground's first consultancy work when an advisory report was requested by the USSR in 1932, and special Order of Lenin awards were made to their British advisors when the Moscow Metro opened in 1935.

The second major project in central London was a new head office for the Underground at 55 Broadway, also designed for Pick by Holden and completed in 1929. At the time it was the tallest office building in Westminster, rising to a central tower ten stories above St James's Park station. Holden came up with an ingenious cruciform plan for the difficult triangular site over the District line station. It gave space for an entrance on both sides to the building and station, connected by a public arcade, and by stepping back the wings up to the tower, all office floors had maximum daylight.

This was London's first American-style skyscraper, though modest in height compared to the towers then going up in Manhattan. Holden commissioned several decorative sculptures for the building exterior by leading modern artists including Eric Gill, Henry Moore and, controversially, Jacob Epstein. The two large

55 Broadway, the new Underground headquarters at St James's Park, completed in 1929, seen at night with floodlighting, c. 1930. This was then the tallest building in Westminster.

Epstein figures at first floor level were criticised by conservatives as primitive and indecent, but the building was awarded the Royal Institute of British Architects (RIBA) London Architectural Medal for 1929. In 2011 Broadway's listed building status was raised to Grade I in recognition of its heritage value and its importance as one of the finest early twentieth-century buildings in London. It is still the Head Office of London Underground.

Before embarking on the next new project to extend the Piccadilly line into the suburbs at both ends, Pick and Holden made an architectural study tour of northern Europe in 1930 to look at some of the latest public buildings they both admired in Sweden, Denmark, Holland and Germany. The new and rebuilt Piccadilly extension stations of 1931–3 north of Finsbury Park and west of Hammersmith include some of Holden's best work, marking the successful evolution of a new and distinctive Underground style. Holden referred to them modestly as his 'brick boxes with concrete lids', but they are very much more than that.

He and Pick had developed a new vocabulary for transport architecture which artfully blended traditional English brick building qualities with modern north European influences, featuring flat concrete roofs and metal framed

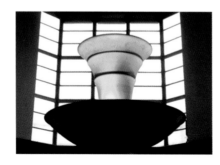

An Art Deco lamp from 1932 still in the booking hall at Bounds Green, a surviving example of Holden's careful attention to detail and fittings in the Piccadilly line extension stations.

windows. The UERL's design style also incorporated the instantly recognisable symbols of the Underground, featuring the bar and circle device, distinctive signage and careful attention to lighting inside and out.

Pick had commissioned a clear sans serif letterface for the Underground from calligrapher Edward Johnston during the First World War, and applied it to most of the UERL's posters and signage from about 1920. Soon afterwards Johnston was asked to redesign the solid red disc station name board as a bar and circle incorporating his lettering. This combination has been used ever since on all Underground stations, with various evolutions and amendments. It also became, successively, the key element in the Underground, London Transport and now TfL's corporate identity. Originally known as the bullseye symbol and today as the roundel, the bar and circle device has effectively become the logo of London itself and is recognised instantly everywhere.

While the UERL established its identity through newly built and modernised infrastructure all over London, Selbie's Metropolitan concentrated on improving its services, structures and equipment throughout its catchment area to the northwest of the city. These were the districts in Middlesex,

Restored direction sign on Edgware Road near Maida Vale station, dating from the 1920s, with Johnston's Underground lettering and redesigned bar and circle symbol.

Hertfordshire and Buckinghamshire collectively known as 'Metro-land', the catchy title devised by one of the Met's publicity staff in 1915 and soon to become almost a synonym for suburbia. Greater London grew faster in Metro-land districts between the wars than in any other area outside the

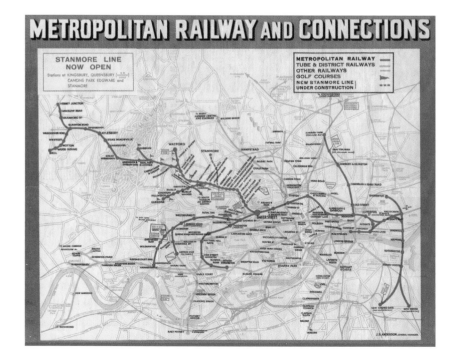

London County Council boundaries. Selbie's company, with its associated housing estate developments, became a very successful commuter railway in this period.

Many of the original Met stations in central and inner suburban London were rebuilt after 1911 to the designs of company architect Charles W. Clark, with distinctive white glazed street facades. Further out in Metro-land, Clark designed new stations in a rather different, domestic style with deep pitched roofs, which blended with the new suburban housing and shopping parades that appeared close to the railway. Electrification of the main Met line was extended from Harrow to Rickmansworth, with a new electric branch to Watford opened in 1925 and a final new line from Wembley Park to Stanmore, opened in 1932.

In 1929, the Met's hub station at Baker Street, by this time grandly promoted by the railway as the 'gateway to Metro-land', was topped off with Chiltern Court, an enormous block of mansion flats, said to be the biggest in London. This too was designed by Clark in a rather heavy Edwardian grand-hotel style which seemed appropriate to the Met's aspirations. Holden's modern head office for the UERL at Broadway, completed at the same time, emphasised the wide stylistic divergence between the two underground companies.

For all the Metropolitan's success in the 1920s, it was clear by the start of the 1930s that it could not survive as an independent operation. The Met had become a curious

Opposite: Metropolitan Railway map, c. 1930, showing the final new construction under way: the Stanmore branch, opened in 1932. London Transport took over the Metropolitan in July 1933.

anomaly with a split personality: half of it was an efficient urban metro but the railway also considered itself a 'mainline in miniature', determined to run everything from luxury Pullman cars to goods trains. In the broader context of London's public transport requirements this no longer made sense. When Selbie died unexpectedly in 1930, the Met lost its leader and champion. Its days were numbered.

What London needed was a single transport authority to run all the city's public transport services. In 1930 there was still a confusing mix of responsibility between public and private management and ownership, which made coordinated transport planning almost impossible. The solution came from one politician, Herbert Morrison, who was Minister of Transport in the 1929 Labour Government. He proposed a new public corporation on the lines of the recently created BBC and Central Electricity Board.

The new Metropolitan station building at Farringdon designed by C. W. Clark in 1923, which included a parcels office. This and the surviving parts of the 1860s station have just been renovated and a new Crossrail station will open as part of this enlarged central London rail hub in 2018.

The London Passenger Transport Board (LPTB) was to be self-supporting and unsubsidised, with a degree of public control but non-political management. Crucially, Morrison got the two key players, Ashfield and Pick of the UERL, on side with his plan, and the LPTB came into being in July 1933. London Transport, as it was soon generally known, took over all bus, tram and underground railway

REFERENCE

DISTRICT RAILWAY		METROPOLITAN RLY
BAKERLOO LINE		METROPOLITAN RLY
PICCADILLY LINE		
EDGWARE, HIGHGATE & MORDEN LINE		EAST LONDON RAILWAY
CENTRAL LONDON RLY		INTERCHANGE STATIONS
		UNDER CONSTRUCTION

H.C. BECK

operation in the Greater London area, but not the suburban services of the mainline companies. They remained separate but agreed to a fare-pooling scheme for their local lines, and to cooperate with London Transport on future developments.

It must have looked like an Underground Group takeover, as Ashfield was made chairman and Pick chief executive of the new authority. The strong and distinctive corporate identity developed by Pick at the UERL using Holden, Johnston and

The first pocket diagram designed by Harry Beck, printed by London Underground in March 1933, a few weeks before the creation of London Transport. This was a seminal moment in graphic design history.

Night view of the new
St John's Wood station
by Holden, Heaps and
LPTB architects,
opened in 1939.

other architects and designers was now expanded and applied to the buildings and equipment inherited from formerly separate organisations that were merged into the LPTB. The Underground, including the Met, was now a single but united department of the largest urban transit authority in the world.

London Transport soon announced a series of ambitious development schemes to modernise and expand its road and

rail services. Under the 1935–40 New Works Programme, London's huge tram network was to be replaced by electric trolleybuses and major improvement works started on the Underground's Metropolitan, Bakerloo, Northern and Central lines. All of these showed the benefits of integrated planning through a single progressive organisation.

Charles Holden was heavily involved in designing London University's large Senate House development in Bloomsbury at this time, and his small architectural practice could not cope with all the new work commissioned after 1933 by the LPTB. Much to Pick's annoyance this meant that many of the new station projects now followed the general Holden style but had to be largely carried out in partnership with other external architects or the LPTB's in-house team. Park Royal (1936), Rayners Lane (1938), Uxbridge (1938), St John's Wood (1939) and East Finchley (1939) are all examples of this – not pure Holden but strikingly modern stations which are all now protected as listed buildings.

A new branch of the Bakerloo line was built in a Tube tunnel below the main Metropolitan line north of Baker Street. It came to the surface at Finchley Road, then ran alongside the fast Met tracks to Wembley Park and took over the Stanmore branch. The Bakerloo service eased congestion on the inner sections of the Met, and was opened in November 1939. Forty years later the Baker Street–Stanmore section became part of the new Jubilee line.

The Northern line was extended from its 1907 terminus at Highgate (Archway), coming to the surface at East Finchley to join the LNER's overground suburban steam branch line built in the 1860s. This was electrified to take new Tube trains through to High Barnet from April 1940. At this stage, when Britain had been at war for just over six months, all remaining parts of the New Works Programme were suspended, some never to be completed. The Underground's boom years were over.

1940–69: WAR, AUSTERITY AND THE VICTORIA LINE

The Underground played a vital role in the Second World War (1939–45), keeping London on the move in difficult conditions as well as providing shelter for thousands of citizens through the bombing raids of the Blitz. Frank Pick was responsible for drawing up evacuation plans for London children at the outbreak of war, and for special precautions and preparations against attack such as watertight doors for the Tube tunnels under the river. He retired from London Transport in 1940 and died in 1941 at a time when much of his life's work was under threat of destruction.

The damage and disruption to the London Transport system was severe but never crippling. A service of some kind could nearly always be maintained, although this was more difficult on the Underground when trackwork and tunnels were hit. As soon as the Blitz started in September 1940, many people took to the Tube for shelter, although this was not officially encouraged and as no special facilities had been installed there were chaotic scenes.

Mass Observation, the social study organisation, reported, 'For the first time in many hundreds of years civilised families conducted the whole of their leisure and domestic lives in full view of each other … most of these people were not merely sheltering in the tubes; they were living there.' This was particularly true in the newly completed Central line extension tunnels east of Liverpool Street. As trains were not yet running here and there was no compulsion for shelterers to leave during the day, many people stayed down for weeks on end, particularly those working-class Londoners who had been bombed out of their homes in the East End and had nowhere else to go.

Gradually, sheltering facilities were properly organised with special admission tickets, bunk beds, refreshments, medical points and, at some stations, libraries, music and live

Sleeping on the escalators at Picadilly Circus when the Blitz began in September 1940. conditions for shelterers were soon more organised, with bunk beds installed on station platforms.

entertainment. The tunnels were not entirely safe from attack, however, and shelterers were killed in six separate incidents when Tube stations were hit.

Underground facilities were also used for military purposes. Brompton Road station, closed in 1934 because it was lightly used, was converted to provide an underground operations room for London's anti-aircraft command. The new Central line tunnels near Redbridge became a secret factory for the Plessey company to build electronic components for military aircraft. A partly built Tube depot at Aldenham for the proposed but unfinished Northern line extension beyond Edgware was adapted to construct Halifax bomber aircraft. At Acton Works, in peacetime the Underground's main repair facility, London Transport overhauled tanks and landing craft motors for the invasion of Europe in 1944.

Plans to resume the interrupted New Works Programme were reviewed in the light of post-war financial difficulties. London Transport faced a massive task of repair and renewal to its bomb-damaged and run-down system. The LPTB was authorised to proceed only with the unfinished eastern and western extensions to the Central line, which were completed to Epping and West Ruislip respectively between 1946 and 1949 in conjunction with the LNER and GWR. The pre-war plans were reduced, with some station reconstruction scaled back or abandoned, leaving many of the stations at the eastern end almost unchanged to receive Tube trains.

A new station for Perivale, on the planned western extension of the Central line, was designed by GWR architect Brian Lewis in 1937, but not built until ten years later.

Gants Hill has a Moscow-style central hall between the platforms. Designed and built in the late 1930s, it was completed and opened in 1947.

The Labour victory at the general election in May 1945 was a prelude to a period of austerity and the nationalisation of key industries and public utilities in the post-war years. In 1947 the LPTB was wound up and London Transport was nationalised along with the four mainline railways to become part of the British Transport Commission (BTC). Lord Ashfield, who had led the LPTB so skilfully as chairman throughout its fifteen-year existence, retired just before the new London Transport Executive (LTE) took over. There was no successor able to live up to his powerful influence and ability.

As just one division of the BTC, the LTE was not high on the government's list for new capital investment. Priority was given to other essential areas of the economy such as house building, electricity generation and the new National Health Service. In public transport the needs of the badly run-down British Railways network outside the capital took precedence.

Coincidentally, in the first year of nationalisation the number of passengers carried by London Transport reached a peak total, but a long decline set in during the 1950s, particularly on the red buses and trolleybuses.

On the Underground all major outstanding projects were abandoned by the early 1950s, notably the Northern line extension schemes. The application of Green Belt legislation killed the justification for building

Loughton station was rebuilt by the **LNER** to a distinctive design by John Murray Easton and opened in 1940. Central line Tube trains first arrived in 1948 when steam services were still operating on to Epping, shown here.

in the countryside north of Edgware, and greater London's population began to fall. The electrification of the line from Finsbury Park to Alexandra Palace via Highgate, although almost completed in 1939, was never carried out and the steam passenger service was closed in 1954.

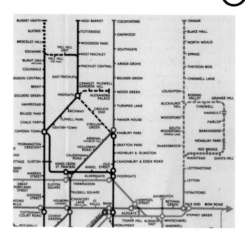

Much of the line is now a pleasant public footpath, along which the remains of the railway infrastructure can still be seen, including the unused electricity sub-station at Crouch End (now a youth club), the abandoned surface interchange station directly above Highgate Tube (rebuilt in 1939–40 but now a ruin), and the original station buildings at the rear of Alexandra Palace itself. It seems unlikely now that Muswell Hill will ever be on the Tube. On the surface railway beyond East Finchley, which had become part of the Northern line in 1940–1, none of the original stations were rebuilt as London Transport had planned before the war.

Detail from the 1947 Tube map showing the new eastern extensions of the Central line (in red) that were soon to open. The planned Northern line extensions (black dotted lines) were soon abandoned.

The only extension of the Tube service in the 1950s came with the electrification of the Epping–Ongar branch in 1957, making this the furthest outpost of the Central line. It was never well used and was eventually closed by London

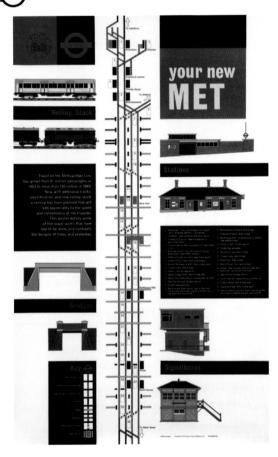

Your New Met. A London Transport poster by William Fenton showing the modernisation taking place on the Metropolitan line, 1960. Moor Park (shown top right) was the only station to be rebuilt as part of this scheme, completed in 1961.

Underground in 1994 and sold, later to be restored as a heritage steam line by a railway preservation group.

Passenger travel on the Underground remained at virtually the same level throughout the 1950s and there seemed no urgent reason to extend the system further, although the long-awaited electrification of the outer Metropolitan line beyond Rickmansworth to Amersham and Chesham was finally completed in 1961. Although the mainline was widened with a new pair of electric tracks, there was little change to the Victorian infrastructure and only one station was rebuilt. Moor Park, given a simple but modern architectural treatment that owed little to the pre-war Holden style, was the first completely new station to open on the Underground since the late 1940s.

Private car ownership boomed in the 1950s, bringing growing traffic congestion in London and a corresponding decline in the reliability of bus services. A new Tube line under central London known as Route C had been proposed in 1949, but was shelved for nearly fifteen years until a cost–benefit study convinced the government that this could very effectively speed up travel across the city.

Renamed the Victoria line, London's first completely new Tube in sixty years was opened from Walthamstow to Victoria in 1968–9, linking five mainline stations and seven Underground lines across the city. An extension opened in 1971 took the Victoria line on to Brixton, the first new Tube south of the river since the completion of the Morden line in 1926.

Although starved of capital investment, the Underground had developed some advanced technology in the 1960s which was skilfully deployed in constructing and operating the new railway. The Victoria line was built in record time, and was the first computer-guided underground railway in the world, with automatic train control based on coded electrical impulses in the running rails. It also had automatic entrance and exit gates opened by magnetically coded tickets. All this chimed with the 'white heat of technology' trumpeted by the Wilson government in the 1960s, though in fact the Victoria line was built to a tight budget and a lower standard of finish than in Pick's period before the war. The design consultants DRU, led by Misha Black, developed a coordinated look for the new stations that was carried through in the unpainted silver aluminium finish of the trains and escalators.

Victoria line northbound platform at Highbury & Islington, 2011. The 1968 tile panels by Edward Bawden are the only decorative features of this depressing station, which has only recently been upgraded at surface level for interchange with the Overground.

Above ground the Victoria line has virtually no surface architecture and little to distinguish the entrances. Inside, the stations are crisp but clinical, decorated only with tile panels on a local theme at intervals along each platform. The Victoria line has not worn well, partly because the quality of materials such as the wall tiles was not up to traditional Underground standards, and soon they got damaged or even dropped off the walls.

The whole line has been refurbished in the early twenty-first century and given a fleet of new walk-through trains. A dramatic new street façade at Brixton with a giant roundel has replaced the original low-key station entrance, but on all the Victoria line platforms upgrades are more muted. The original tile designs above the recessed seats are still the only features that give the stations some individuality and it seems unlikely that DRU's 'cool Sixties' style will justify any future heritage listing.

Victoria line platform at Euston, designed for London Transport by consultants Misha Black and DRU and completed in 1967. Tom Eckersley's tile panels reference the famous Euston Arch, controversially demolished by BR five years earlier for the rebuilding of the mainline station above.

1970–99: TO HEATHROW IN THE WEST AND DOCKLANDS IN THE EAST

Responsibility for London Transport was transferred to the Greater London Council (GLC) in 1970. Transport in the city became a political and environmental issue as finding ways to stop the private car destroying London through urban motorways and redevelopment schemes gained momentum. Bigger and wider road schemes were not the answer but neither, it seemed, was renewed investment in the Underground. Every new development in this period seemed penny-pinching and inadequate, while London

Transport became a political football with little vision and weak management.

Rather late in the day, Heathrow Airport, already the busiest in the world, was given a direct rail link to the city centre through an extension to the Piccadilly line in 1977. This was later extended with a loop to serve new Heathrow Terminals 4 (1986) and 5 (2008). The slow Tube route to central London eventually had to be augmented by a fast but expensive overground rail service to Paddington – the Heathrow Express, opened in 1998. Twenty years beyond that, another service to Heathrow will become available with the completion of Crossrail in 2018.

Hatton Cross station on the Heathrow extension, a bland London Transport design from 1975 which still looks bleak today.

In design terms the various Tube stations on the Heathrow extension are fairly bland and unexciting with minimal decoration. Hatton Cross (1975), on the edge of the airport, is the only one with surface buildings and a bus interchange alongside. It is a good spot for watching planes but a very dull, functional environment, typical of London Transport's declining design standards in the 1970s.

Instead of capitalising on the success of the Victoria line, London Transport was only authorised to build stage one of the next new Tube under central London. The new section of the Jubilee line, opened in 1979, was a short extension from Baker Street to Charing Cross of the existing Stanmore branch of the Bakerloo opened forty years earlier. There were no new surface buildings, although the new entrance to Bond Street was incorporated in a small retail mall which left the Tube with no street presence except a tiny roundel. Frank Pick would have been horrified.

In contrast to the clinical interiors of the Victoria line, booking halls and platforms were given brightly coloured decorative schemes devised by London Transport's architects' department. The most successful of these were carried through a large part of the refurbished underground areas at Baker Street, with a Sherlock Holmes decorative theme on new tiling and platform wall panels. Even more striking are the former Strand and Trafalgar Square station platforms at Charing Cross, where the refurbished Northern and Bakerloo line platforms were given full-length decorative wall panels. More than thirty years on these design features still look very stylish.

Stage two of the Jubilee line, taking it south and east to Docklands rather than

Baker Street Jubilee line platform, opened in 1979. London Transport's architects introduced brightly coloured station decoration in reaction to the dull greyness of the Victoria line. The panel on the right is a Sherlock Holmes illustration by Robin Jacques.

through the City as originally planned, was not completed until twenty years later in 1999. Meanwhile the general state of the Underground deteriorated further in the 1980s, with an increase in crime, litter and graffiti across the network. A few central stations such as Tottenham Court Road were given a much-needed makeover, in this case using brightly coloured mosaic designs by Eduardo Paolozzi, but overall the Tube felt neglected and in decline.

Despite its poor condition, patronage of the Tube had begun to grow rapidly in the mid-1980s. The bitter 'Fares Fair' battle between the GLC and central government over the legality of subsidising London Transport fares led to the government taking back direct control of the buses and Underground, and eventually abolishing the GLC altogether. A more positive outcome for Londoners was a simpler zonal fares system and the Travelcard, both of which encouraged much greater use of the Tube.

But this was against a background of decline, which led to the Underground's lowest point: the serious fire at King's Cross station in November 1987, in which thirty-one people died. The immediate cause of the tragedy was a smoker's match dropped on to a poorly maintained wooden escalator, but the public enquiry exposed a culture of management

Mosaic tile designs by Eduardo Paolozzi at Tottenham Court Road, applied throughout the station as part of a refurbishment programme in the mid-1980s. These have always been controversial, both loved and hated.

complacency and inadequate staff fire safety training. It was a terrible wake-up call for the Tube, and the poor practices revealed by the Fennell enquiry report in 1988 forced London Underground to confront its weaknesses and work towards creating a system that was safer, more resilient and one that London could rely on. A complete overhaul of safety systems and a determined refurbishment and clean-up of the entire network was undertaken in the 1990s under new management. The Underground had to become, in new managing director Denis Tunnicliffe's phrase, 'a decently modern metro'.

The DLR and new Docklands development, looking east from the hub station at Poplar, 2010.

The key project that spearheaded the Tube's recovery in the 1990s was the Jubilee line extension (JLE), eventually to be London Underground's greatest achievement at the close of the twentieth century, despite being delayed and well over budget. Phase two of the Jubilee line had effectively been abandoned during the political and financial battles of the early 1980s. At the same time the early proposals for regenerating London's Docklands were to use a cheap and cheerful automated light railway network rather than an expensive new Tube as public transport.

When the initial Docklands Light Railway (DLR) opened in 1987 it was plagued with failures and problems with the computer control systems which were to require major upgrades and the virtual reconstruction of the network. Meanwhile, the Canary Wharf scheme, which was promising to create at least 50,000 jobs in a giant new business centre at the heart of the isolated Isle of Dogs, suddenly changed the transport requirements for the area.

The fortunes of Canary Wharf and the Jubilee line extension became inextricably linked in a rollercoaster of boom and bust in the 1990s. The property developers were originally to contribute one third of the cost of the new railway but after the financial crash of 1992 it became the government's commitment to the JLE that saved Canary Wharf and underpinned its recovery when construction of the line started in 1993.

The 10-mile JLE was on a revised route linking Westminster with Stratford in east London via Southwark and Docklands, but not the City as originally planned. London Underground set out to learn from the Victoria and Jubilee line experience, and from the King's Cross fire, but also, as London was no longer in the vanguard, from the latest metro-building overseas. London Transport's

Bermondsey Jubilee line station, designed by Ian Ritchie Associates and opened in 1999. Like all below ground stations on the JLE it has platform edge safety doors which only open when a train has arrived and stopped.

The dramatic main entrance to Canary Wharf Jubilee line station by Norman Foster, opened in 1999. The glass canopy is an enlarged version of the standard entrances he designed for the new Bilbao Metro in Spain, known locally as 'Fosteritos'.

new chairman from 1988 was Sir Wilfrid Newton, recruited from the Mass Transit Railway (MTR) in Hong Kong, one of the most advanced and successful modern metros. He brought in Roland Paoletti, chief architect of the MTR, to oversee the design of the JLE.

The new stations were made as spacious as possible below ground, sitting in massive concrete boxes. Features included step-free access, dual exits at both ends of station platforms for safe evacuation, smoke ventilation systems, platform edge doors, fireproof lifts and at least three escalators at each station.

Paoletti did not design the structures himself but commissioned several external architectural practices to work with his team on each of the eleven new stations and the Stratford Market train depot. It was quite different to the Pick/Holden approach but the result was creative variety and quality architecture within a very strong and coherent overall design vision, bringing architects and engineers together at every level. 'Even Holden didn't get below ground,' said Paoletti, 'the architecture ran out in the ticket hall'.

Without question the JLE represents some of the finest modern public design in late twentieth-century London, though when it opened in 1999 its legacy was obscured by cost over-runs and delays. The most serious problem was the failure to introduce automatic train operation and the new

The DLR station at Canary Wharf was enlarged and rebuilt as soon as the system opened in 1987, when the huge scale of the planned business centre was announced. The present station, with four platforms and an overall roof, was opened in 1991.

moving block signalling system to enable improved train frequencies. This took another twelve years to achieve, with regular failures and weekend closures during the lengthy upgrade. Now the JLE can run up to thirty-three trains per hour, it soaks up passengers at peak times, and it has been key to the further regeneration of Docklands and east London, including the 2012 Olympics. The DLR, once derided as a toytown railway in its early days, has become the fastest growing and most reliable line in the country, linking the Tube with a much wider area of east and south-east London.

2000–19: PPP, OVERGROUND AND CROSSRAIL

The Labour government elected in 1997 set up a new city-wide authority for London, to be led by an elected Mayor, whose biggest financial responsibility would be transport, including London Underground (LU). Transport for London (TfL) was created in 2000, replacing London Transport but taking on much wider responsibilities including taxis, riverboats, the DLR, Tramlink, cycling and streets as well as bus services and the Tube.

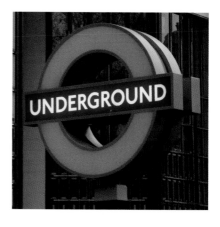

1990s-style roundel at South Kensington, 2012.

A sticking point in carrying out the transfer was the proposed funding mechanism for the continued maintenance and modernisation of the Underground. The government had decided to set up a Public Private Partnership (PPP) to do this, committing TfL as the public authority to thirty-year contracts with private consortia, who would be paid to carry out the agreed upgrade work. The first elected Mayor, Ken Livingstone, was forced to accept a complex and fatally flawed method of funding the Tube that nobody fully understood.

Contracts were signed with two newly created infrastructure companies (Metronet and Tubelines) in 2003 but by 2007 Metronet had collapsed and in 2010 Tubelines was dissolved with all work returning to in-house management. As a means of financing the Tube's ongoing costs, PPP was abandoned and quietly paid off, an embarrassing and very expensive failure. LU is now an integrated public company again, still part of TfL and responsible to the London mayor at City Hall, not the government at Westminster.

There has been a far more strategic approach to transport planning in London since the creation of TfL and mayoral governance. Despite the financial crash of 2008 and the onset of recession, passenger numbers on the Tube are at record levels with more than 1.2 billion annual journeys. Most of these are now made using Oyster smartcards, introduced in 2003, which have revolutionised payment and ticketing across all travel modes in the city.

Opposite:
London City Airport station on the DLR Woolwich extension, opened in 2006.

Two major rail development projects linked to the Underground, but not actually part of it, have got under way in the twenty-first century. They will both help to meet new travel needs and increase overall capacity on London's public transport. The first is London Overground, created by TfL in 2007 to manage some suburban rail services transferred from the national network. These had been run down and neglected for many years, particularly the old North London line, which had once been a busy commuter railway. For the first time since the Victorian era the benefits of running orbital passenger services across London's inner suburbs, linked to radial routes through the centre, were recognised.

By reinstating and upgrading old routes and creating new links at both ends of the fully refurbished and extended East London line, a complete orbital metro network was created, opened in stages between 2010 and 2012. It runs through twenty of London's thirty-three boroughs, and 30 per cent of Londoners now live less than fifteen minutes' walk from an Overground station. London Overground has a fleet of new trains and much-improved

Haggerston, a new station on the extended East London line designed by Acanthus LW architects with a retro nod to Holden's pre-war style, 2010.

Tiled mural design at Haggerston, opened as part of London Overground, 2010.

services, with a similar but distinct branding to the Underground. In effect this has put large areas of London which have never had an Underground station – such as Hackney, Peckham and Sydenham – 'on the Tube'.

All of the former Network Rail stations have been refurbished and rebranded by TfL, just as London Transport did to the LNER surface stations taken over for the Northern and Central line extensions in the 1940s. Where completely new stations have been built, such as Hoxton and Haggerston, these have the quality of the best modern urban design but also make a gesture back to Holden's classic Tube stations of the 1930s.

Crossrail, a far more ambitious project, is a joint venture between TfL and the Department of Transport to build a new railway right under London linking Heathrow and Maidenhead

Cutaway impression of the multi-level Crossrail station at Canary Wharf, now under construction in a giant concrete coffer dam built within the former West India Docks. Crossrail is scheduled to open in 2018.

in the west with Shenfield and Abbey Wood in the east. New tunnels will take high-frequency mainline-size trains deep below central London, with Tube interchange at seven new stations between Paddington and Canary Wharf. It will be the London equivalent of the Paris RER lines built in the 1970s, which are separate from the city's Metro but linked to it.

This huge and costly project was first proposed over twenty years ago and, like the Victoria and Jubilee lines, is only going ahead after many years of planning, debate and eventual government authorisation to spend public money. Tunnel boring began in 2012 and construction is now due for completion in 2018. Crossrail will be, in effect, London's next Tube, but on a mainline scale.

Transport for London's wider responsibilities have made it easier to integrate services across the whole spectrum of travel, and to plan future developments on a broad scale that old London Transport was unable to achieve. Since 2000, both of London's elected mayors have used their transport powers to promote the city's economic, social and environmental development. For all the political wrangling, the Underground in particular is now recognised by all sides as the key to London's future success and sustainability. It is still, as Frank Pick put it in the 1930s, 'the framework of the town'. Harry Beck's iconic Underground map, which now incorporates the Overground and DLR networks, is the perfect representation of this. Use it for your journeys of exploration.

TUBE JOURNEYS

Here are seven suggested journeys through which to explore the Tube, including examples of the best station architecture and design from the last 150 years – these are highlighted in bold in the text. The routes are best followed with the current pocket Tube map, which is available free at every London Underground station, as an app for mobile devices, or can be downloaded from the TfL website.

As well as the Underground network, the map includes Overground, DLR and Emirates Air Line routes. All of these accept Oyster card payment, although an all-zones Travelcard is recommended as the cheapest way to do two or three of these journeys in a day if you are planning to leave stations and pass through ticket barriers. The journeys can be made in any order but each will take two or three hours to complete. Remember that Harry Beck's iconic design offers a diagrammatic representation of the Underground, not a geographical map, and both time and space are distorted. Stations appear to be the same distance apart when in fact they are widely spaced in outer London and close together in the centre. This makes it easy to read but deceptive.

Opposite: East Finchley, rebuilt in 1939–40 for the Northern line extension to the designs of Holden and Bucknell. The station's most striking feature is the lead-coated archer figure by Eric Aumonier, now a north London landmark.

The Tube can be busy and crowded at virtually any time of day, but travel outside the weekday peaks of 7.30–9.30 a.m. and 16.00–18.30 p.m. is recommended, especially for central areas. Do not use flash photography or a tripod anywhere inside a station, and particularly on platforms, escalators and trains.

Holden-designed 1930s roundel seat at High Street Kensington, still an elegant and practical piece of station furniture in everyday use today.

INNER CIRCLE

Start at **Paddington** (Hammersmith & City), site of the original Metropolitan Railway station opened in 1863, called Bishop's Road, on the north side of the GWR's mainline terminus. It was completely rebuilt and enlarged in 2011–12, with a new entrance/exit to the Paddington Basin and Central developments beside the canal.

Take an eastbound train to **Baker Street**. The Circle line platforms here are still in the original brick arched cut-and-cover tunnel below the Marylebone Road, cleaned and renovated in the 1970s with replicas of the original globe gas lighting. Walk towards the exit at the end of the platform, where an elaborate marble war memorial (on the left) has stood since 1920, restored and rededicated in 2010.

You can explore the rest of Baker Street station on the Metro-land trip. For now, take an eastbound train over the original 1863 section of the Met via King's Cross to **Farringdon**. This station is being rebuilt and expanded in the twenty-first century, but still has listed features dating back to the 1860s, notably the train shed over the Met and former 'widened lines' now used by Thameslink services. The old booking hall, rebuilt in 1915 by Met architect C.W. Clark with one of his white-glazed tiled

The Metropolitan and Circle line platforms at Farringdon, still under the 1860s train shed, with Thameslink platforms beyond the columns.

street exteriors, has just been renovated and additional station exits added. A new linked Crossrail station will open

Farringdon Street station in 1868 after completion of Fowler's train shed, which remains today. The steam train has arrived on the 'widened lines' from Moorgate or on the cross-river link from south London through Blackfriars opened in 1866.

Farringdon in the
evening peak looking
towards the City,
January 2012.
St Paul's Cathedral
is in the centre and
beyond left are the
lights of the Shard
tower at London Bridge,
nearing completion as
the tallest building in
Europe. A Crossrail
station will open
underneath Farringdon
in 2018.

under the current plaforms in 2018, when Farringdon will become a major hub and interchange.

Continue east on a Circle line train. Get off at **Temple**, on the southern side of the Circle, originally built by the District Railway along the new Thames Embankment and opened in 1870. The original cast-iron support columns survive at platform level, but at street level the station was rebuilt after electrification to a design by Harry W. Ford, the company architect, in 1914–15. It is a long, single-storey building in Portland stone, intended to match Somerset House nearby on the Embankment.

Refurbished roundel at Temple on an original support bracket from the time when the station was rebuilt by H. W. Ford in 1915.

The next station, **Embankment** (originally Charing Cross), was also rebuilt by Ford in 1914, with interchange below ground to the new Bakerloo and Hampstead (now Northern line) Tubes, both part of the UERL. The white-enamelled steel wall panels on all platforms at Embankment were designed by Robyn Denny, and installed when the whole complex was renovated in 1988, brightening up the station but also being easy to clean at a time when the Underground environment was suffering its first serious graffiti tagging. On the surface, the pediments above the two street

Temple station as rebuilt
for the District Railway
in 1915 by Harry Ford to
match the style of nearby
Somerset House.

Jacob Epstein's *Day*
on the façade of 55
Broadway, controversial
in 1929 but hardly
noticed today.

entrances to the booking hall originally carried large
mosaic Underground symbols, since removed. Ford
claimed to have designed the original solid red
bullseye symbol and UNDERGROUND lettering
first introduced in 1908.

St James's Park platforms are in the tiled
white, green and black design used on many UERL
stations in the 1920s, well preserved here because
the building above is 55 Broadway, the company
head office designed by Holden and completed in
1929. It is worth walking through the interior
arcade (adapted in the 1980s to close off the
reception area) and then all round the exterior to

Gloucester Road station in 2012, with the restored frontages of the 1868 Metropolitan District building (right) and the 1906 Piccadilly Tube station (left).

look at the details both close up and at a distance. Epstein's *Night* and *Day* figures are at first floor level on the two main façades, but you will need binoculars to see the other decorative sculptures by Eric Gill, Henry Moore and others high up on the building.

Gloucester Road station was where the Metropolitan and District lines first joined up in 1868, sharing the station but remaining separate companies. Part of the station was rebuilt and rafted over in the early 1990s, though given a heritage rather than a modern design style. A disused platform is used to present art exhibitions against the brick retaining wall. At street level the original two-storey 1868 building designed by John Fowler has been restored, with the renovated frontage of the Piccadilly Tube station alongside, which was designed by Leslie Green and opened in 1907.

Take a District line train to **Earl's Court**, which has design features from several periods. The current District line station with its large overall roof dates from 1878, when this area of west London was first being developed with new housing on what had been market gardens. The train shed was recently renovated and new platform lifts fitted, but some early twentieth-century features were retained, including the original electric train describers dating from about 1905 and the combined wooden seats with roundel nameboards from the 1930s.

The Piccadilly Tube arrived at Earl's Court in 1906 with platforms directly below the District, both railways having become part of Yerkes' UERL. A new joint entrance and booking hall was built, designed by H. W. Ford, with lift access to the Piccadilly, and in 1911 the first escalators on the Underground linked the District and Piccadilly platforms. The other end of the station was rebuilt and extended in the late 1930s to serve the new Earl's Court exhibition halls opened in 1937. This is all by London Transport architects in the

Earl's Court station 2012, under the original train shed designed by District Railway engineer John Wolfe Barry in 1878. The 1905 train describers (bottom right) and 1930s roundel platform seats have been kept in the recent renovation and upgrade.

Holden house style of the LPTB, and includes an escalator shaft with its original bronze column uplighters, one of only three remaining on the system (the others are at Southgate and St John's Wood). The underground passage to the exhibition centre was used as the LPTB's 'spare time' factory during the war.

Take a District line train to **High Street Kensington**. Opened by the Metropolitan in 1868, this station was modernised in the 1900s and 1930s, and features survive from both periods. An entrance arcade from the High Street with shop windows and covered access to the adjacent department stores of Pontings and Derry & Toms was

The station arcade at High Street Kensington with art nouveau decoration, designed by George Sherrin for the Metropolitan after electrification, c. 1907.

The original 1868 train shed at Paddington (District & Circle) station, designed by the Metropolitan's engineer John Fowler and opened as Praed Street on the Metropolitan extension to link up with the District at South Kensington.

opened in 1907, designed by the Met's consulting architect George Sherrin. His elegant arcade and octagon has survived, though the original shops have not. The LPTB built a new booking hall here in Holden style in 1937 and added to the platforms below some of the stylish but practical roundel seats also seen at Earl's Court.

Our journey ends at **Paddington**. The current District & Circle station was built by the Metropolitan as part of its western extension, opened in 1868 and originally called Praed Street to distinguish it from the first Met station at Bishop's Road, where we started. Much of the original train shed, the standard design for this part of the line, still survives here, but the booking hall and Praed Street façade were rebuilt by C. W. Clark in 1915. Cross the road to enjoy the interior of the Great Western mainline station with its magnificent triple-span roof, designed by I. K. Brunel in 1854. The fourth span (to the right), was added in the same style in 1916. There were plans to raft over this for office development above the station, but fortunately these were abandoned, and the roof has recently been carefully restored and cleaned. It now looks superb.

PIONEER TUBES

This tour includes developments on the Underground from the first Tube in 1890 to the most recent completely new station on the system, opened in the twenty-first century.

Start at **Paddington**, travelling west on the Hammersmith & City (H&C) line, a joint overground development by the Metropolitan and Great Western Railways, opened in 1864. Get off at **Wood Lane**. This is a brand new station opened in 2008 and given the same name as the original H&C line station nearby, which closed in 1959. The impressive modern station was designed by Ian Ritchie Architects and is clad entirely in stainless steel, anodised aluminium and granite panels with a 25-metre high, glass-screened façade to the street. It was built to serve the giant Westfield shopping centre nearby.

At the bottom of the steps from the platform, under the arch on the left, is a restored mosaic roundel. This was rescued from the façade of Wood Lane Central London Railway (CLR) Tube station nearby, built in 1908 to serve the White City exhibition site, but closed when the new White City station was opened in 1947. It lay derelict until final demolition for the Westfield development.

Turn left outside the station and walk under the bridge. The Westfield shopping centre is on the left just beyond the bus station, which incorporates part of the original red brick power house for the CLR built for the new electric Tube in 1900.

This pre-dates the much larger power station at Lots Road, Chelsea, built by Yerkes for the UERL in 1902–5, which superseded it in the 1920s. The structure survived, was given protection as a listed building, and has found a new use, housing buses instead of power turbines.

Retrace your steps along Wood Lane past the station to **White City** Central line station, just along the street opposite the BBC Television Centre. This station was designed in Holden style by London Transport architects in 1946 as part of the Central line extension programme, which was suspended because of the war in 1939. It has a spacious glass-fronted booking hall, designed to take the crowds attending greyhound racing and other sporting events held at White City before the BBC took over the site in the 1960s. A blue plaque on the street façade announces that the station won a Festival of Britain design award in 1951. This was to be the last example of quality architecture on the Underground until the Jubilee line extension stations opened nearly fifty years later.

Take an eastbound train one stop to **Shepherd's Bush**, the original western terminus of the Central London Railway opened in 1900. At platform level the tile designs reflect the refurbishment of the Central line carried out in the 1980s. On the surface the original station was

The new station at Shepherd's Bush, which replaced the original 1900 Central London Railway building in 2008 as part of the planning gain from the Westfield shopping centre alongside.

completely rebuilt in 2005, funded by the developers of the Westfield shopping centre. The surface buildings were completed in 2008, with a new station on the London Overground line opening over the road at the same time.

Return to the Tube and head towards central London. Get off at both **Holland Park** and **Queensway** to see restored examples of the original CLR surface buildings of 1900. All the station entrances from Shepherd's Bush to Bank followed a standard design by Harry B. Measures. Each one had single-storey terracotta tiled street frontage with potential for lettable office space to be added on top. Holland Park station, still in a residential area, remains closest to its original appearance with no upper floors. At Queensway, facing Kensington Gardens across the street, apartments were soon built over the station after it opened in the early 1900s. A century later the whole station, including the street façade, was sympathetically modernised as part of the station upgrade programme.

Change at **Tottenham Court Road** to the southbound Northern line. All underground areas of this station were cosmetically refurbished in the early 1980s using bright and colourful mosaic tiling designs by Eduardo Paolozzi inspired by the photographic, music and electronic products for which this

Central London Railway station façade at Queensway in matt terracotta with original lamp brackets, designed by Harry B. Measures in 1900, refurbished in 2007.

Detail from the decorative mosaics at Tottenham Court Road, designed by Eduardo Paolozzi, 1983.

Charing Cross Northern line platform-length murals on warerite panels, 2009. Designed by David Gentleman in 1979 and looking good thirty years on.

area is known. As a reminder of TCR's previous grubby state see the Tube scene in *An American Werewolf in London,* filmed in 1979, where the beast stalks a victim through the run-down station. TCR is now being extensively enlarged and rebuilt in connection with the development of Crossrail, which will open an interchange station with the Tube here in 2018. Some of the Paolozzi mosaics will have to be relocated or recreated in the process.

Take a train to **Charing Cross**, stopping to admire the superb platform-length mural decorations designed by

David Gentleman in 1979, which tell the story of the medieval cross put up here by King Edward I to commemorate his wife Queen Eleanor when she died in 1290. The black-and-white figures are enlarged from wood engravings made from boxwood blocks, and screenprinted onto the wall panels.

Travel on to **Kennington**. The surface building here, now listed, is the only survivor of the original domed structures designed by Thomas Figgis for the pioneer Tube line, the City & South London Railway, opened in 1890. Just down the line at **Clapham Common**, which became the C&SLR's southern terminus in 1900, is the last surviving narrow island platform in a single deep tube station tunnel. This rather alarming arrangement, where you can experience standing between two fast-moving trains travelling in opposite directions, was also used at Angel until the station was rebuilt with twin tunnels in 1992.

All seven stations from here to **Morden,** on the UERL extension opened in 1926, have surface buildings designed by Charles Holden, each one a variation on the three-leaf entrance kiosk he designed for **Clapham South** in 1925. They are all similar, with a Portland stone and glass façade featuring prominent Underground roundels, but the layout varies according

Platform at Kennington, opened in 1890, rebuilt around 1924 with new tiling and electric clock, then refurbished around 2004. The original City & South London Railway domed entrance building by Thomas Figgis survives on the surface, the oldest Tube station in London.

Stockwell, the original south London Tube terminus, as opened in 1890 with electric locomotive-hauled trains, gas lighting and a single wooden island platform. The station has since been completely reconstructed above and below ground.

Clapham Common, the last surviving underground island platform in a single Tube tunnel, built in 1900.

to the site from a tight angled entrance at **Tooting Bec** to a wide curve at **Tooting Broadway**. These stations must have looked astonishingly modern when they opened, and represent the first successful move towards a distinctive corporate style for the Underground which Pick and Holden developed together in the inter-war years. Return to central London by Tube when you have visited at least two of the Morden extension stations for comparison.

Colliers Wood, one of Charles Holden's innovative angled screen entrance kiosks in Portland stone and glass for the Morden extension stations, 1926.

BRINGING CHICAGO TO LONDON: THE YERKES TUBES

This journey looks at the three Tube lines built by the American transit mogul Charles Tyson Yerkes (1837–1905) as part of his Underground Electric Railways of London (UERL). These are the Bakerloo, Piccadilly and Hampstead (now Northern) lines opened in 1906–7. Yerkes' business methods were devious and underhand, but he proved to be the only person capable of completing the London Tube network, though he died before any of the new lines were running.

Start at **Elephant & Castle**, southern terminus of the Bakerloo from 1906. The surface building here is a well-preserved and typical example of the standard stations designed for the UERL Tubes by Leslie W. Green. Not surprisingly, both the structural and electrical engineering of the UERL's three Tubes follow American ideas and practice. Every one of Green's forty-plus stations was built in the same way, on a load-bearing steel frame which could take the weight of the heavy lift motors and winding gear as well as upper-floor lettable office space above the station itself. This was the building method for high-rise construction pioneered in Chicago, but barely used in Edwardian London. At Elephant & Castle three floors of offices were added immediately above the two-storey station structure.

Tiled 'Way Out' signs were used at all the UERL stations of 1906–7. This modern replica of an original is at Covent Garden.

The station is clad in glazed, ox-blood coloured terracotta blocks called faience. These blocks could be moulded to different designs but were effectively mass-produced by the Leeds Fireclay Company at their Burmantofts pottery. Similar, but not identical, materials were supplied for each station, giving the buildings a strong corporate identity as well as a consistent colour scheme.

All the original UERL stations of 1906–7 had a similar interior design, with extensive use of coloured tiling and elaborate green faience surrounds to the ticket windows. Every station had at least two American Otis electric lifts, with Art Nouveau decoration on the doors and ventilation grilles. All the original lifts have been replaced but some of the decorative features survive in the booking hall here and elsewhere.

Take the lift to the platform level. Each Yerkes station has a unique coloured tiling pattern along the platforms to help identification from the train. The original station names were fired into the tile decoration at either end and in the centre of each platform. This inadequate system was soon replaced from 1908 onwards by bar-and-disc nameplates and later by an enamel frieze repeating the name all along the platform. Poster advertising soon covered up much of the wall tiling.

Continue through to **Regent's Park** station, which has recently been renovated with a partly replicated tiling scheme to restore its 1906 appearance. There was never a surface building at this station but some examples of the original decorative lift grilles have been retained in the modernised sub-surface booking hall.

Edgware Road was fully renovated in heritage style in 1992. The platforms have been retiled to the 1906 pattern, incorporating the original station name tiling at either end. The Leslie Green surface

Retiled platform in the style of the original 1906 design at Regents Park, 2009.

Maida Vale on the Bakerloo Tube extension, opened in 1915. The station was designed by Stanley Heaps, Leslie Green's assistant, who succeeded him as UERL architect in 1908. There are well-preserved mosaic roundels over the stairs just inside the entrance.

booking hall has convincingly replicated ticket window surrounds and partial heritage lighting. This was one of the prototype heritage upgrades which were initiated after the King's Cross fire, incorporating new ticket gates, safety systems and signage.

Continue to **Maida Vale**, one of the stations on the Bakerloo extension completed during the First World War. When it opened in 1915 the station was the first to be entirely staffed by women. Leslie Green had died in 1908, and all extension stations on the UERL were designed by his former assistant Stanley Heaps, who became the Underground's architect until 1933 and was the LPTB's in-house architect until 1943, working with Holden and others as external consulting architects.

Maida Vale is less florid than Green's original stations, with a simpler entrance hall design but continuing the use of ox-blood faience on the façade. Inside, above the entrance staircase from the street are two fine mosaic-tiled Underground symbols similar to the earlier external designs used at Embankment (originally Charing Cross) and Wood Lane.

Return on the Bakerloo to **Charing Cross** (formerly Trafalgar Square station), which was extensively refurbished and rebuilt in 1979. Picture details from the National Gallery and National Portrait Gallery nearby are reproduced on mural panels all along the Bakerloo platforms, which still look very effective more than thirty years later. Change to the Northern line, also stylishly redecorated in 1979 with David Gentleman's medieval Eleanor Cross designs.

The Bakerloo platforms at Charing Cross (originally Trafalgar Square) were decorated with designs taken from paintings in the nearby National Gallery in 1979.

Take a northbound train to **Mornington Crescent**, the first of the Hampstead Tube stations of 1907 to be given a comprehensive heritage

Original 1907 lift exit doors and ventilation grilles with Art Nouveau decoration, restored at Mornington Crescent station in the 1990s.

The long wraparound façade of Chalk Farm station by Leslie Green for the Hampstead Tube, opened by the UERL in 1907.

restoration in the 1990s. After a six-year closure it was reopened in 1998 by the cast of the popular BBC Radio 4 comedy panel show *I'm Sorry I Haven't A Clue*, which has long featured a game named after the station. A memorial plaque to the late Willie Rushton, one of the longest-serving panellists, was put up in the booking hall in 2002.

Take an Edgware branch train to **Chalk Farm**. The 1907 surface building here is in Green's usual style but adapted to a tight street junction layout which gives it the longest continuous façade of all the Yerkes stations. It is elegantly wrapped round a corner prow of the building, facing central London and the restored Roundhouse performing arts centre, originally built as an engine shed in Camden for the London & Birmingham Railway.

Take the Tube to **Hampstead**, another 1907 station by Green of standard design but distinguished by being the deepest in London. The platforms are 58.5 metres below ground level. You might like to try using the emergency spiral staircase to the surface which has 320 steps. The original proposed station name, Heath Street, is fired into the platform wall tiles.

Continue northbound, looking out on the right for the ghost station platform at North End (often referred to as Bull & Bush), constructed in the tunnels but never completed with passenger lift shafts or a surface building. This is one of the unexplained mysteries of the Tube system that has given rise to much ill-informed speculation about its later potential role as a deep shelter or control centre, for which it was never converted.

Golders Green was the original surface terminus and depot of the Hampstead Tube when it opened in 1907, creating the first Underground suburb on what were then green fields at a country crossroads. Much of the original station remains, smartly modernised and renovated in the twenty-first century with replicated tiling on the stairs and passageway, and restored platform canopies. With the large bus station in the station forecourt this is still one of the main transport hubs for north London, as it became a century ago.

METRO-LAND

This is a journey up the Metropolitan Railway's 'extension line' from Baker Street, taking in part of the Jubilee line originally built as a relief line to the Met and opening as a branch of the Bakerloo in 1939.

Start with an exploration of the **Baker Street** complex, always referred to by the railway in the 1920s as the Gateway to Metro-land. The Metropolitan & St John's Wood Railway was built as a feeder line to the original underground, opening to Swiss Cottage in 1868 and extended overground as part of

No longer a Luncheon &
Tea Room, but much of
Baker Street's main
booking hall concourse,
designed by C. W. Clark
for the Metropolitan
Railway in 1911, has been
preserved and renovated.
Chiltern Court, above the
station and also by Clark,
was not completed
until 1930.

the Metropolitan right out to Harrow by1880, then on to Amersham and Aylesbury in 1892.

After electrification in 1905, Baker Street station was extensively rebuilt to provide better interchange and a proper junction with the 'mainline' to the northwest. The Circle line platforms were left unmodernised but the rest of the station was rebuilt and extensively altered between 1910 and 1925. This included the large booking-hall concourse, just below ground level along the Marylebone Road frontage, where refreshment rooms, cloakrooms and other improved passenger facilities were installed. The cream-tiled façade to the Luncheon and Tea Room can still be seen, now framing the wall ticket machines and a cash dispenser.

There were plans to build a large hotel over the station frontage but these were abandoned during the First World War. Eventually the Chiltern Court luxury apartment block rose over the Marylebone Road frontage in the late 1920s. It was completed in 1929–30, when H. G. Wells and Arnold Bennett were among the early tenants. Chiltern Court had its own restaurant on the ground floor, now a pub retaining much of its original décor. All this was designed by the Met's architect C. W. Clark, in a rather traditional Edwardian style fondly evoked by John Betjeman in his poem 'The Metropolitan Railway, Baker Street Buffet', written in 1954.

Take an Uxbridge line train to **Ruislip**. The branch from Harrow to Uxbridge was opened by the Met in 1904, initially as a steam service but with new electric trains from the end of the year. Ruislip, near the village centre, is the only stop on the line with its original building, a traditional country railway station more in keeping with the Victorian age than the dawning twentieth century, but it hardly changed over the next century.

Continue to the terminus at **Uxbridge**, a new station opened in 1938 on a site closer to the old town centre than the original Met station of 1904, which no longer exists.

Opening day of the Uxbridge branch at Ruislip, 1904. The original station building here survives, as does the steam locomotive, Met no. 1, now based at the Buckinghamshire Railway Centre and restored to work special commemorative services for the 150th anniversary of the Underground in 2013.

Uxbridge Underground station, built by the LPTB on a new High Street site in 1938. Designed by Holden with Leonard Bucknell and sculpture decoration by Joseph Armitage.

The station was designed for the LPTB by Holden with Leonard Bucknell and opened in 1938. The concrete train shed is a development of the Cockfosters design completed in 1933, with a curved forecourt containing a shopping parade. Above the entrance are sculptures based on stylised train wheels by Joseph Armitage and in the arcade below are stained glass windows by Ervin Bossanyi with the coats of arms of Uxbridge, Middlesex and Buckinghamshire.

Take any train back to **Rayners Lane**. Suburban development was slow all along the Uxbridge branch, and the line was not well used until new Metro-land housing developments took off in the late 1920s. The new housing estates built close to Rayners Lane station, a remote spot with little more than a farm and a rifle range when it opened in 1904, were rebranded as Harrow Garden Village in 1929. The station was soon at the heart of a new semi-detached suburban community with shopping parades and a large Art Deco-style cinema. The rapid increase in passenger numbers made station reconstruction necessary when the LPTB took over in 1933. A large new station building designed in Holden style by Reginald Uren was completed in 1938, by which time the branch was served by extended Piccadilly line services

Rayners Lane station as rebuilt by the **LPTB** in 1938, to the designs of Reginald Uren in the Holden house style.

over the former District South Harrow branch as well as fast Metropolitan line trains from Baker Street.

Take a Metropolitan train to **Wembley Park**, a station successively rebuilt and enlarged since the Empire Stadium and British Empire Exhibition put Wembley on the map in the early 1920s. The iconic concrete sports stadium, home of English football, was finally demolished and rebuilt by the FA as a larger venue in 2003, prompting another station reconstruction to handle the bigger football crowds that now attend matches. The large new entrance building on the stadium side was completed in 2006.

Take a northbound Jubilee line service to **Stanmore**. This was the last new branch opened by the Metropolitan Railway in December 1932, months before it was taken over by London Transport. The terminus at Stanmore is in Clark's domestic style with deep-pitched roofs redolent of a small Arts and Crafts country house, especially when viewed from the platforms at the top of a steep flight of steps.

Get off at **Kingsbury** on the way back to see the same domestic station design fitted into a shopping parade at street level, and blending comfortably with the suburban housing that sprang up around the new railway in the 1930s. Queensbury was the chosen name in a competition to name the next new community and station on the line, opened by London Transport in 1934.

Take the train to **Willesden Green**, first opened by the Metropolitan in 1879. The main station building at street level was rebuilt in 1925 to Clark's 'city' design in the white

Willesden Green, rebuilt in 1925 for the Metropolitan in Clark's earlier urban style with a cream faience exterior as seen at **Aldgate**, **Farringdon** and other central London stations. This is the best-preserved example, still featuring some 1920s mosaic tiling in the booking hall.

faience style used for his reconstructed booking halls at urban sites like Farringdon, Edgware Road and Paddington. Willesden Green was the farthest of these designs from central London and is now the best preserved, standing prominently on the main road over-bridge. In comparison with Holden's contemporary designs for the UERL's Morden extension stations, Clark's work here is fussy and over detailed but it is a striking contribution to the suburban landscape. Notice the mosaic-tiled interior, stripped out from most of Clark's other stations, and the diamond-shaped exterior clock on a bracket, also removed from other stations.

Take the southbound Jubilee line, which runs overground alongside the fast Metropolitan lines to the interchange station at Finchley Road, where it enters a Tube tunnel. Get off at **St John's Wood**, opened as a new Bakerloo Tube station in 1939. The whole station, which has recently been refurbished, is in the standard LPTB house style developed by Holden in the 1930s. The lower concourse and platform areas have biscuit-coloured tiling throughout, including a station name frieze and randomly applied tiles with a series of decorative relief designs by Harold Stabler of Poole Pottery.

St John's Wood, originally opened by the LPTB on the new Bakerloo extension in 1939, modernised in heritage style in 2005. These are modern escalators fitted with bronze uplighters designed by Holden in the 1930s.

The 1930s escalators have been replaced but the original uplighters and hanging globe lights have been kept. The semicircular booking hall has been renovated but the station's original appearance from the street has long been spoiled by the unsympathetic block of flats built on top of it in the 1960s. Turn right and walk a short distance up the road to see the former Metropolitan **Marlborough Road** station building on the corner of Queen's Grove. This was closed when the Bakerloo Tube station opened nearby in November 1939, and has been a restaurant since the 1970s. Met trains still run through the abandoned Marlborough Road station platforms below.

Return to St John's Wood station and take the Jubilee line back to **Baker Street**. The deep-level areas of Baker Street were originally a separate Bakerloo Tube station opened in 1906. They were partly reconstructed with escalators replacing the lifts in the late 1930s when the new Bakerloo branch was built, then rebuilt again in the 1970s for the transfer to the Jubilee line. All the lower concourse and platform areas were given decorative motifs associated with Baker Street's famous fictional resident, Sherlock Holmes. New tiling was applied throughout in 1979 and on the Jubilee line platforms wall panels were installed, with illustrations in period style by Robin Jacques from the Conan Doyle detective stories.

Sherlock Holmes tiling at Baker Street, 1979.

NORTHERN HEIGHTS

This is a round trip on the Northern line from central London up the original Highgate branch of the Hampstead Tube, which became the High Barnet branch with the link to the electrified steam suburban lines in 1939–40. This part of the 1935–40 New Works Programme was suspended because of the war and never completed afterwards.

Start at **Leicester Square**, one of the Hampstead Tube stations opened in 1907. The original Leslie Green street façade survives on Charing Cross Road but the station was completely reconstructed below ground in the 1930s by the LPTB, with a circular sub-surface booking hall and escalators instead of lifts to the Northern and Piccadilly lines. The new subway entrances from the street have 1930s-style roundels above the steps, and biscuit-coloured wall tiling trimmed with a unique LT border motif which does not appear anywhere else on the system. Take the Northern line escalators. At platform level this station was refurbished again in the 1980s with wall tile designs decorated with film sprocket holes to represent the West End cinema district around Leicester Square.

Highgate, completed in 1939 under the New Works Programme, refurbished and retiled to the original designs, c. 2005.

Take the Northern line High Barnet branch to **Highgate**, the next station beyond the 1907 Tube terminus at Archway (originally called Highgate). The extension was built under the 1935–40 New Works Programme, which brought the Tube to the surface at East Finchley. The new Highgate Tube station was opened in 1939 directly below the old LNER steam suburban station on the surface, first opened in 1867. The low-level platforms, recently refurbished with new tiling replicating the 1930s design, are unusually long and were designed to take nine-coach trains which were initially proposed for the 1938 Tube stock. In practice these units were always run as seven-car trains.

The old surface station above Highgate Tube was partly rebuilt in the 1930s with new platform canopies in readiness for the electrification of the Finsbury Park to Alexandra Palace branch line and Tube operation as another addition to the Northern line. This work was well advanced when it was suspended in 1939 but never completed after the war. The high-

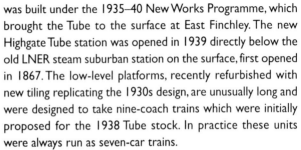

level station can still be seen, fenced off and gradually decaying. Much of the route from Highgate through Muswell Hill to Alexandra Palace, and in the other direction through Crouch End to Finsbury Park, now forms the popular Parkland Walk, which makes an interesting diversion at this point if you have time.

Return to the station and take a train to **East Finchley**. The Tube extension reached the surface here in 1939, joining

Highgate surface station in 2007. Rebuilt in 1940 for proposed interchange with the new **Northern** line station below, but never completed, it is slowly returning to nature.

the overground line from Highgate used by LNER steam suburban services. East Finchley was completely rebuilt to take LPTB Tube trains as a large four-track interchange station, designed by Holden with L. H. Bucknell and opened in 1939. This is now the finest and most impressive station on the Northern line, still topped with Eric Aumonier's Art Deco archer figure symbolically speeding the trains towards London.

Tube services were running through to **High Barnet** by 1940, and on the branch to **Mill Hill East** in 1941, but further development work was stopped during the war, never to be restarted. The original intermediate stations at **Finchley Central**, **Woodside Park** and **Totteridge & Whetstone** became Tube stations with nothing more than electric conductor rails, new colour light signalling and London Transport station signs. Otherwise they remain practically unchanged from steam days, though recently spruced up and with some new facilities inserted, such as a passenger lift at Finchley Central and a new booking hall at West Finchley.

Having explored the High Barnet branch you can return to Finchley Central and change to a **Mill Hill East** train which will cross the tallest brick viaduct on the Underground, built high over the Dollis Brook by John Fowler at the same time

Woodside Park, a Great Northern Railway branchline station built in 1872. Electric Tube trains arrived in 1940, giving the line rapid access to the City and West End, but other than Underground branding, the Victorian station has hardly changed and has been beautifully renovated.

Edgware station in the late 1920s. All five Hampstead Tube stations on the extension north of Golders Green were designed by UERL architect Stanley Heaps in this neo-Georgian style and opened in 1923–4. Brent Cross is the least altered.

as he was supervising construction of the original Metropolitan Railway in the 1860s. The line originally continued through Mill Hill to Edgware but was never electrified beyond Mill Hill East. This final part of the New Works Programme, with a Tube extension beyond Edgware to Bushey Heath, was not completed after the war when Green Belt legislation was applied to Greater London.

You can either return to central London on the Northern line direct from Mill Hill East or take a 221 or 240 bus to **Edgware** for a trip down the earlier extension of the Hampstead Tube, from Golders Green through Hendon, completed in 1923–4. This Tube extension was the principal spur to the suburban development of Middlesex all down the line in the 1920s and '30s. All five of the new stations were designed by Stanley Heaps in an Italianate style best represented today by **Hendon Central** and **Brent Cross**, which have been altered least. Edgware itself has lost its original courtyard wings.

PICCADILLY PROGRESS

This journey consists of two separate trips from central London over the extended Piccadilly line created in the early 1930s to look at some of Charles Holden's finest station designs in the classic Underground style he developed for Frank Pick.

Start at **Piccadilly Circus**, the station redeveloped by the UERL in the mid-1920s as the heart of the Empire and showpiece hub of the London Underground. The circular booking hall effectively reproduces below ground John Nash's original Regency circus at the intersection of Regent Street and Piccadilly, which had been lost in Victorian and Edwardian redevelopment. Holden's design recreates the elegance of Nash in a modern context underground.

The station was extensively refurbished in the 1980s with features

The oval booking hall at Piccadilly Circus, the UERL's showpiece station at the heart of London, rebuilt in 1925–8. Design features like the world map (left) and Holden's hanging lamps were refurbished in the late 1980s, when the lower concourse and platform areas were retiled and modernised.

Covent Garden by Leslie Green for the UERL, opened in 1907. The interior at street level has been remodelled but at lower and platform levels new tiling in 2008 has replicated the original designs.

such as the world clock retained and the hanging lamps of the 'ambulatory' restored while the unsympathetic fluorescent strip lighting of the 1950s was removed. The lower concourse and platform areas were brightened up with a new tiling scheme that did not attempt to imitate the past.

Take the northbound Piccadilly line. Some of the original stations of 1906–7 have been sympathetically upgraded more recently with restored or replicated heritage features. These include **Covent Garden**, **Russell Square**, **Caledonian Road** and **Holloway Road**.

Arsenal station platform in 2010, with new tiling replicating the 1906 style and pattern, including the original name Gillespie Road, changed in 1932.

Arsenal, which has also been renovated, is the only London Tube station named after the local football team, a change made in 1932 when the Gunners were the top London club but had already been at Highbury for twenty-one years, having moved from Woolwich in 1913. The original station opened in 1906 was called Gillespie Road, now revealed in the restored platform tiling. Arsenal moved to their new Emirates stadium in 2006, which is actually closer to Holloway Road station, though Arsenal is still more convenient for match crowds because it is off the main road and has passageways rather than lifts to the shallow Tube platforms.

The Piccadilly line was extended north of Finsbury Park in 1932–3. All eight of the new stations were designed by

Arnos Grove, widely considered to be Holden's best Tube station, completed in 1932. The drum on a cube form of the booking hall is similar in style to Erik Asplund's celebrated city library in Stockholm (1924–7), which Pick and Holden both admired.

Southgate station by night when first opened in 1933, looking as if a futuristic flying saucer has landed in an old village, yet instantly creating a new focal point for the growing suburb. Another of Holden's classic designs.

Charles Holden both above and below ground. No two are identical but each incorporates the features of his Underground house style at its peak, clearly influenced by the north European civic architecture he and Pick had admired on their study tour in 1930. It is worth getting off the train to explore every station beyond Finsbury Park inside and out, but if your time is limited, the best stations to see are the four outer stations at **Arnos Grove, Southgate, Oakwood** and **Cockfosters**, which demonstrate Holden's skill at providing variety within a strong and effective corporate identity. All are now listed and have been carefully restored but are still 'fit for purpose' in Pick and Holden's phrase, functioning beautifully as busy working stations. Arnos Grove and Southgate are among the finest examples of new commercial architecture built in

London in the 1930s and were acclaimed as such at the time.

Take the Tube back through central London to look at the Piccadilly extension stations at the western end of the line. Get off at **Hammersmith**, the original 1906 terminus. The joint station with the District was rebuilt in Holden style when the Piccadilly was extended westwards alongside the District

tracks in 1931–2. It was rebuilt again by London Underground in the early 1990s as part of a commercial property development scheme incorporating a shopping centre, bus station and office complex. Within this the station has retained a distinctive character that makes visual reference to Holden's scheme of sixty years earlier, including reproduction 1930s roundel seats on the platforms and architectural fragments of the 1906 station façade by Harry Ford reassembled in the booking hall.

Take a Piccadilly line train over the western extension to **Sudbury Town**, Holden's 1931 prototype for his 'brick box with a concrete lid' style which replaced the old District Railway station of 1903. This was the most radical new station design in the country at the time, quite different from anything on the mainline railways.

At the new Piccadilly line terminus at Cockfosters, completed in 1933, Holden reshaped the familiar Victorian arched iron train shed in reinforced concrete and glass. Uxbridge, built at the other end of the line five years later, has the same basic design.

Holden expanded the massed brick, concrete and metal-framed window elements of this style in the rebuilt stations at **Sudbury Hill** and **South Harrow**, just up the line. This former District branch, opened in 1903, was transferred to Piccadilly operation with new Tube trains in the 1930s.

Before returning to central London, get off at **Park Royal** to see the Holden-like new station designed for London Transport in 1936 by Welch & Lander, architects of the adjacent Hanger Hill estate, which has houses, flats and a shopping parade in a complementary style. This is the best of the 'nearly Holden'

Sudbury Town, Holden's prototype 'brick box with a concrete lid', soon after opening in 1931. It replaced the very basic corrugated iron station building put up by the District Railway when the line opened in 1903. The stylish uplighters do not survive.

stations, designed by other architects in the late 1930s in the Holden style when his own architectural practice was unable to carry out all the new work required by the LPTB. Pick was unhappy that these stations did not get Holden's personal supervision but the results were still to a very high standard.

Other western extension stations designed by Holden in the early 1930s worth visiting if time allows are **Chiswick Park** on the District line and **Acton Town**, **Northfields**, **Boston Manor** and **Osterley**, the last three on the Heathrow branch.

Park Royal, designed for the **LPTB** in Holden style by **Welch & Lander**, architects of the adjacent **Hanger Hill** housing estate and shops in 1936.

The roof and windows inside a typical Holden box station after refurbishment, 2011. **Acton Town**, rebuilt in 1932–3, is similar but not identical to other contemporary designs on the Piccadilly line such as **Sudbury Hill**, **Northfields** and **Oakwood**.

Return to central London and get off at **Green Park** to see the latest developments on the Piccadilly. This station opened in 1906 as Dover Street but was completely rebuilt in 1933, with escalators, and renamed because it had new subway entrances right on Piccadilly at Green Park. The Victoria and Jubilee lines also served Green Park from 1969 and 1979 respectively.

Thirty years later work began on another major upgrade to make Green Park the first fully accessible deep Tube station in central London in time for the

New low-level 'green' entrance to **Green Park** station, 2012. There is a lift from street level under the new canopy on the south side of Piccadilly, making this the first deep Tube station inside the Circle line with a step-free route from street to train.

2012 Olympics. This meant providing step-free access with lifts and ramps from ground level to train on all three tube lines. This work was completed on schedule and includes a completely new fully accessible ramp and lift entrance to the station. The ramp from the ticket hall leads directly into the park and there is a stylish modern canopy above the staircase and lift on the south side of Piccadilly. The new street structures have fossil artworks within the Portland stone cladding designed by artist John Maine. These latest features at Green Park are very much in the spirit of Pick and Holden, practical but beautifully designed contributions to the public realm in London.

HEADING SOUTH AND EAST: DLR AND JLE

This journey is mainly through parts of east London where the development of the Docklands Light Railway (DLR) and the Jubilee line extension (JLE) have reshaped the landscape of Docklands and the wider eastern side of the city.

Take the Central line east from anywhere in central London to **Bethnal Green**. The eastern extension beyond Liverpool Street was largely constructed by 1939 but not completed and opened until after the war. The long, deep tunnel section under the East End was used as a civilian bomb shelter during the war, and it was at the unfinished Bethnal Green station that one of the worst incidents occurred. On 3 March 1943, 173 people were crushed to death on a stairwell to the station shelter when a mother carrying a baby tripped in the dark and others fell on top of her. This tragic incident is commemorated in a new memorial outside the station.

The Central line service through Bethnal Green started in 1946 when the station was fitted out for operation. It has recently been fully renovated with the replication of 1930s tiling and the restoration of

Bethnal Green station, designed and built in 1938–9, was used as a shelter during the war but not completed and opened until 1946. It was refurbished with new replica tiling and the original roundel clocks restored in 2005–6.

the stunning original platform clocks, which have roundels for numerals.

Continue to **Stratford**, first reached by Tube trains in 1946. This has had surface interchange with mainline services since then, and the station has been expanded and rebuilt over the last twenty-five years to include two DLR lines, JLE and Overground services. The Olympic Park and Westfield shopping centre occupy former railway lands on one side of the station, which have required additional entrances and access facilities to be built since 2005, making this the busiest new transport hub in east London.

After exploring the station complex, take the DLR line towards Canary Wharf. The DLR does not have much exceptional design on its own system but it does offer the best way to see the transformation of Docklands and, because much of it is elevated, the finest views of east London, particularly on the Beckton and Woolwich lines. Most of the stations have basic system-built structures, but it is worth getting off at **Langdon Park** to see one of the latest new stations added to the system in 2007. The distinctive modern design is by Consarc Architects.

Langdon Park DLR station by Consarc architects, opened in 2007, with the towers of Canary Wharf in the distance.

Change at **Poplar**, the main hub of the DLR, to ride the elevated branch lines further east. You should finish your DLR journey at **Royal Victoria**. Get off here to take the Emirates Air Line cable car high above the Thames from Royal Docks to the Greenwich Peninsula, a trip with even more spectacular views over the river. Change to the Jubilee line at **North Greenwich**, the station built to serve the adjacent Millennium Dome, now the O₂.

View looking west from Pontoon Dock DLR station, 2010. The roof of the O2 dome at North Greenwich is in the centre with Canary Wharf beyond.

The construction of the JLE in the 1990s marked London Underground's return to high-quality architecture on a par with Holden's work in the 1930s. The stations were designed by various architectural practices commissioned and overseen by chief project architect Roland Paoletti who co-ordinated the work of different designers, architects and engineers with the project team. It was the biggest combined architectural and engineering project ever undertaken by London Underground, complex and costly but a spectacular achievement when it was completed in 1999. Paoletti wrote of the JLE in 2000 that 'the route and stations of the extension effectively link Victorian construction with the modern world and propel both into the future'.

Every one of the eleven JLE stations is worth a visit because each is different but contributes to the whole. If you have the time, visit them all, but if your first exploration is limited, see the following at least.

You are starting at **North Greenwich**, designed by the JLE project architects with Alsop, Lyall & Stormer. The linked bus station is by Foster & Partners. The unique character of North Greenwich lies in the contrast of stainless steel and blue mosaic running throughout the station at every level, with ceilings 'unfinished' and services deliberately exposed.

Take the Jubilee line to **Canary Wharf**. The JLE station here serves the huge commercial development built on part

The vast cathedral-like main hall of Canary Wharf Jubilee line station, designed by Norman Foster, ready for opening in 1999. It sits in a huge concrete box below ground level in the former dock.

The glazed drum of the Canada Water transport hub reflected in part of the former Surrey Docks, 1999. This Jubilee and East London line interchange station was designed by the JLE project architects and the bus station by Eva Jiricna Architects, completed in 1999.

of the redundant West India Docks. It sits in a giant concrete box within a former dock basin which has enabled the station to be built on an enormous scale in contrast to the traditional confined underground spaces of the Tube. Norman Foster's station combines engineering strength and architectural elegance, transforming the box into a spectacular concrete-vaulted environment, which, despite its immense volume, feels comfortable and inviting. This is still the only London Tube station where there is space for commuters to queue for their train in the evening rush hour, lining up at each platform edge door for a few minutes but rarely longer.

Take the train to **Canada Water**, a transport interchange in the former Surrey Docks where the JLE station also serves London Overground's East London line and there is an integrated bus station designed by Eva Jiricna architects. The structure of the JLE station is in exposed concrete with a glazed central drum rising out of it, a design nod to Holden's Arnos Grove. Change on to a northbound London Overground service if you want to explore the Thames Tunnel and the extended East London line to Hackney, reopened in 2010.

If continuing on the JLE get off to look at **Bermondsey**, designed by Ian Ritchie Architects, a welcoming station in a clean

The dramatic lower concourse at Southwark Jubilee line station, designed by MacCormac, Jamieson Prichard and JLE project architects and opened in 1999.

concrete box where natural light fills the escalator shaft and filters right down to platform level. This has brought the Tube to Jamaica Road, an area with no previous rail links to central London. Two stops further on is **Southwark**, also serving an inner London area south of the river but not previously near the Tube. The two lower concourse areas of this station, designed by Richard MacCormac, make particularly good use of contrasting materials: stone, glass and silver metal panelling juxtaposed in different shapes and volumes.

Inside the main exposed box of Westminster station, designed by Michael Hopkins & Partners, who were also architects for Portcullis House, the new parliamentary building above the station, all completed in 1999.

Leave the JLE at **Westminster**, an engineering triumph where the station had to be shoehorned into the lower part of a deep box excavated around the existing District line platforms without stopping the train service. Michael Hopkins was architect both for the JLE station and Portcullis House, the new parliamentary building which sits on top of the station. He left the 40-metre deep box between the two largely open with the escalators running through the void between beams, pipes and the structural supports of the offices above, like a high-tech classical vision by Piranesi. This is the most extraordinary space of all, the exposed interface of architecture, design and engineering at the heart of London, an appropriate place to end our final journey.

FURTHER READING

This book is a brief introduction to the London Underground. A vast amount of detailed information about the history, stations and operation of the network is available both online and in print. Here are some suggestions for further exploration:

BOOKS

Badsey-Ellis, Anthony. *The Hampstead Tube*. Capital Transport, 2007.

Bayman, Bob. *Underground Official Handbook*. Capital Transport, 2008.

Bownes, David, Green, Oliver and Mullins, Sam. *Underground: How the Tube Shaped London*. Allen Lane, 2012.

Bownes, David and Green, Oliver. *London Transport Posters: A Century of Art and Design*. Lund Humphries, 2008.

Bruce, J. Graeme and Croome, Desmond. *The Twopenny Tube*. Capital Transport, 1996.

Connor, J. E. *London's Disused Underground Stations*. Capital Transport, 2001.

Croome, Desmond F. *The Circle Line*. Capital Transport, 2003.

Croome, Desmond F. and Jackson, Alan. *Rails through the Clay: A History of London's Tube Railways*. Capital Transport, 1993.

Day, John R. and Reed, John. *The Story of London's Underground*. Capital Transport, 2010.

Dobbin, Claire. *London Underground Maps: Art, Design and Cartography*. Lund Humphries, 2012.

Edwards, Dennis. *London's Underground Suburbs*. Capital Transport, 2003.

Emmerson, Andrew. *The London Underground*. Shire Publications, 2010.

Emmerson, Andrew and Beard, Tony. *London's Secret Tubes*. Capital Transport, 2004.

Glover, John. *London's Overground*. Ian Allan, 2012.

Halliday, Stephen. *Underground to Everywhere: London's Underground Railway in the Life of the Capital*. Sutton Publishing, 2001.

Harris, Cyril. *What's in a name? The Origins of Station Names on the London Underground and DLR*. Capital Transport, 2001.

Horne, Mike. *The Jubilee Line*. Capital Transport, 2000.

Horne, Mike. *The Bakerloo Line*. Capital Transport, 2001.

Horne, Mike. *The Metropolitan Line*. Capital Transport, 2003.

Horne, Mike. *The District Line*. Capital Transport, 2005.

Horne, Mike. *The Victoria Line*. Capital Transport, 2004.

Horne, Mike. *The Piccadilly Tube*. Capital Transport, 2007.

Jackson, Alan A. *London's Local Railways*. Capital Transport, 1999.

Jackson, Alan A. *London's Metro-land*. Capital Transport, 2006.

Lawrence, David. *Underground Architecture*. Capital Transport, 1994.

Leboff, David. *London Underground Stations*. Ian Allan, 1994.

Pearce, Alan, Hardy, Brian and Stannard, Colin. *DLR Official Handbook*. Capital Transport, 2006.

Pedroche, Ben. *Do Not Alight Here: Walking London's Lost Underground and Railway Stations*. Capital History, 2011.

Powell, Kenneth. *The Jubilee line Extension*. Laurence King, 2000.

Wolmar, Christian. *The Subterranean Railway*. Atlantic Books, 2004.

WEBSITES

www.ltmuseum.co.uk

www.tfl.gov.uk

www.urbandesign.tfl.gov.uk

www.crossrail.co.uk

www.londonrailways.net

INDEX OF STATIONS